THE STUDENT

A Guide To Success In Second And Third Level Education

By

DR. MARY DINEEN M.B., F.R.C. Psych., D.PM.
and
DR. BREDA C. McLEAVEY M.A., Ph.D.

Folens

Acknowledgements

The authors would like to express their gratitude to Sara Dineen, Student, University College Cork, for her strong support with this book. Her research on diet, physical exercise and the practicalities of dealing with the examination itself was much appreciated.

We thank Dr. William Reville, University College Cork, for his considerable help and advice on scientific aspects of the book.

Our thanks to Dr. Robin Godfrey, Medical Director, Student Health, University College Cork, who kindly provided the survey on third level students.

We are grateful for the support of those teachers in second and third level colleges who provided guidance and encouragement. Their suggestions on current difficulties encountered in education were particularly helpful.

Our thanks to the following Clinicians whose expertise and comments were most welcome: Dr. B. McCaffrey, E.H.B.; Dr. S. O'Cathail, S.H.B.; Dr. B. Delaney, E.H.B.

We are indebted to Mr. Noel McCarthy and Brian Murphy of Bridge Co-Op., who distributed and collected the numerous surveys in second level colleges in Cork city and county.

Finally, our thanks to Emma Dineen, Student, University College Cork, for her constant criticism. Her view on orals, aurals and MCQs, together with her work on statistics was gratefully accepted.

ISBN 086 121 4609

Editor: Anna O'Donovan

Layout and Design: Teresa Burke

Artwork: Caroline Taylor, Katharine White

© **1992 Folens Publishers**, Airton Road, Tallaght, Dublin 24, Ireland

Contents

Foreword

This is a delightful book, full of positive practical advice. How I wish I had such a volume available to me during my own student days. It is written in clear, crisp language with copious examples, gleaned from wide and immediate experience.

The advice is not only practical but is based on well established psychological and medical principles. The style is friendly and encouraging, with emphasis throughout on positive and healthy attitudes leading to a balanced, healthy lifestyle.

The encouraging message to the student is:

You can take control of your life as a student;
You can handle the tension and stress;
You can turn the pressures of examinations to your advantage;
You can organize your time and study;
Time can become your friend rather than an elusive enemy;
You can become a more relaxed and healthier person;
Here are tried and tested skills and techniques to help you.

The advice to parents and teachers is equally encouraging and positive. The authors share very generously from their experience as parents and also from their professional involvement in student health over many years. While pitfalls are pointed to, the overall emphasis is to enable our young people to live their student lives to the full and to enjoy them. Questions and issues addressed in a simple straight-forward manner include: how to study effectively; how to solve problems; how to handle anxiety; examination nerves; healthy habits; diet; exercise and relaxation; alcohol; drugs, etc.

I feel very happy to recommend this book to parents, teachers and students alike. It is a real 'Vade-mecum', a guide, counsellor and friend. It is a most timely contribution to the health, well-being and success of students.

Br. Bede Minehane

Irish Provincial of
The Presentation Brothers

INTRODUCTION

This book is written to help the adolescent and the young adult to cope with the pressures encountered in the second and third level educational systems.

Educational matters aside, the period from early teens to early twenties is a difficult period in one's life. During this period great physical, psychological and emotional changes occur as we mature from children into adults. These changes are natural and inevitable. They are also challenging and can be difficult to cope with. Most people go through these changes without great difficulty. Some do not, and there are many opportunities to make wrong choices. On top of this vulnerable time of change, there is an educational system which puts the student under a significant amount of added pressure.

By educational system we do not solely mean the framework of classroom, teachers, syllabus, exams and points system. The parent's and student's attitude to education and their expectations of education are also part of the system.

For various reasons there is more pressure on today's student than was felt by his/her counterpart in the past. At the same time, opportunities to escape these and other pressures are more plentiful than ever before. Students have more money than they had in the past, and society is more tolerant of certain behaviours at much earlier ages than it used to be, e.g. teenage drinking, late night parties, etc. In the cities and towns various drugs are available to those who seek them. Opportunities and pressures to go astray abound. Of course, there is no shortage of people to point out to young people what is wrong, and therefore what to avoid. However, in itself this can only have a limited effect. In many cases this advice is delivered in the form of preaching in a high moral tone and this is counter-productive. What young people need is, not a list of things to avoid, but a recipe for positive living and thinking. This is what we have attempted to provide in this book.

The book looks at many of the stresses encountered by the student. It shows how to handle difficulties in a healthy and controlled way. Straightforward answers are given to questions such as, "How should I organize my study? How long should I study? How should I prepare for examinations? How should I handle examination nerves? How should I solve problems? What sort of exercise should I take and how much? What is a healthy diet? Should I take a drink, and how much drinking is appropriate and safe? Should I experiment with drugs?" etc. All the answers and guidelines are based on tried and tested psychological and medical principles.

Handling the pressures of the educational system and adolescent development is not difficult when approached in the right way. We hope that this book will be a valuable guide to students and also to their parents.

Dr. Mary Dineen qualified in Medicine in 1970 and she has worked in psychiatry ever since. She is a consultant psychiatrist with the Southern Health Board and a lecturer in psychiatry in University College Cork. For many years she has been involved with the Student Health Department at University College Cork.

Dr. Dineen is married with four children, two in second level and two in third level education. She was awarded Fellowship of the Royal College of Psychiatrists in 1987.

Dr. Breda McLeavey is a graduate of University College, Cork, and Iowa State University. She has been a Clinical Psychologist with the Southern Health Board since 1979, and is also a College Lecturer in the Department of Psychiatry, University College, Cork. She was involved in the development and organization of the Social and Health Education programme of Ogra Chorcai, for secondary schools. She provides lectures and workshops on stress management to a wide range of groups and organizations. She is currently very active in the area of suicide research, and has developed an internationally-used problem-solving skills training programme for young suicide attempters.

Dr. McLeavey is married with two school-going children.

1. STUDY SKILLS

By the time students get to senior second or to third level, many have developed attitudes and approaches to study that impede, or sometimes block their path to success. The enemies of academic success are:

- A negative attitude to work
- Lack of goals and priorities
- Unrealistic goals
- Attention/concentration problems
- Poor planning and last-minute cramming
- Chronic social or emotional problems

1. MOTIVATION

The impetus to strive toward achievement and success is developed over a lifetime, but develops particularly during childhood and adolescence. Temperament, home environment, parental and other role models, and school experiences, are just some of the many factors that enhance or impede this aspect of personality development. As one moves up through the educational system one meets ever-increasing academic demands, and with fewer external controls on study (parents and teachers become less involved in monitoring and checking work), motivation becomes the cornerstone of progress. It is not possible to succeed without a good level of motivation. It is possible, however, to increase your motivation level by developing a positive attitude to work and by setting realistic goals.

STUDY IS HARD WORK

HARD WORK IS PART OF LIFE

There is no doubt that study is demanding and that it can be difficult. But to see study as tedious, as a necessary evil, as infringing on your freedom, is to miss the chance of really enjoying student life.

Work is an essential part of the human condition at all stages. It is an important mechanism whereby we grow in self- esteem and in spirit, and whereby we contribute to the good of society at large. Education is the appropriate work of young people. At each stage you have grown further in knowledge and wisdom, forming the foundation of a productive and fulfilling adulthood.

While study is demanding and often difficult, like any worthwhile activity it brings its own rewards – a sense of satisfaction and achievement at having done your best.

YOUR GOALS

The most important factor in keeping up your motivation to work is having goals. Without goals you are prey to competing attractions (e.g. avoiding/skipping "boring" classes/lectures to meet a friend, going to the bowling alley instead of on the history trip to the museum), to being easily convinced by the views and behaviour of others, and to lack of structure and purpose. It is difficult to start into a study session and to stay at it if you do not really know the purpose of the work in the first place. So it is essential to have

- Long-term goals
- Medium-term goals
- Short-term goals

Long-Term Goals

The aim of any education, whether second or third level, is not simply to prepare for "a good job". That is why it is not sufficient to just read textbooks and carry out assignments. The social, sporting and other areas of life as a student are extremely important and certainly shouldn't be neglected. However, there is no doubt that one of the primary aims of the educational system is preparation for a future career. It is when you begin to have some definite ideas as to the career you might wish to have that you will find satisfaction and purpose in your work.

So take an active interest in your future vocation, talk to people involved in it, and relate as much of your study as possible to getting there.

Medium-Term Goals

Once you see a long-term reason for your work, i.e. your future career, you will want to ensure that you do your best at each stage getting there. Medium-term goals are, therefore, mostly to do with doing well in exams, projects, establishing priorities, etc. You need a good Leaving Certificate to get into college or to get the best job available. You need to get your degree before you can apply for any professional post. So your primary aim becomes a good approach to study. Other areas are secondary. This allows you to set your priorities with study as number one.

Short-Term Goals

There are times when immediate distractions (a phonecall, a friend drops in, a good T.V. programme) compete strongly with the weekly plan. But you know what you want to achieve in any one week, and at the start of a study session you should know what you want to have completed by the end of it. These are your short-term goals and you must give them top priority. This means that you should deal with distractions in the shortest possible time and should re-schedule any that you can deal with outside of study time. It is important to write out a job list for each day (e.g. buy notebook, tidy garage, ring John) and to fit these in when time is available. If something occurs to you while studying – write it down to be attended to later. This allows you to dismiss it from your mind without the worry that it might be forgotten.

Realistic Goals

Having goals makes life more exciting and study more interesting and rewarding. But your goals should be realistic. Setting them too high will lead to disappointment and frustration, and eventually to viewing your studies as irrelevant and not worthwhile. Past performance is your guide for goal-setting. You should always aim a little higher than your last achievement so that you give your best. If you have been getting 40 - 50% try for 50 - 55%. But if you have been getting a low pass all along in a subject, and it takes a lot of extra time and effort to get a high pass mark in this, stay with the pass course – don't try for honours. Consider a career that is within the reach of your best performance, even if this rules out a profession that you would really like. There are many jobs related to your choice of career that demand different levels of results. Consider everything before narrowing down your preferences.

Setting goals too low is also detrimental to success. There are many reasons why students do this, e.g. peer pressure to be like the others, fear of being thought of as a "bore" or "swot", lack of encouragement by family members, or fear of failure. You must deal with pressures and worries instead of letting them stand in your way. Seek out people who will give you the extra encouragement you need to pursue your interests – teachers, students who enjoy or do well in that subject, relatives or friends who have knowledge or interest in it. Your time as a student is relatively short in your overall life-span. These years belong to you and it is your responsibility to make the most of them. If you sell yourself short by setting your goals too low you will have plenty of time to regret it later. At each stage you should reach a little higher than you have been achieving. If you go down in marks at any point, don't be discouraged. This is a learning opportunity. Welcome the comments and criticisms of teachers/tutors to improve your knowledge and your performance. Look for regular feedback on your work to help you to judge how well you are working toward your medium and long-term goals.

2. ATTENTION AND CONCENTRATION

Attention is the capacity to focus on one thing while screening out others that are present to the various senses (noises, sights, smells). For example, while you are bringing a small child across a busy street you focus on the traffic and disregard the child's questions, the people on the footpath, the smell of exhaust fumes, your sore toe, etc.

Concentration is purposeful, heightened attention, sustained over a period of time. You decide what to attend to, put effort into doing so, and keep up this deliberate focus until the task is complete.

Ability to concentrate is a pre-condition for effective study. Some students are more easily distracted than others. If you find it difficult to settle at any one subject for very long, or get very little done over study periods, you need to build up your capacity to concentrate. There are a number of angles to this:

- Good planning
- The right environment
- A good start
- Length of individual study units
- Managing distractions

GOOD PLANNING

This is essential for concentration. Without it your attention is divided between what you are doing and what you should be doing and worry about what is not getting done. The Master Plan and the Weekly Timetable are discussed in Chapter 2. On your weekly timetable you should schedule in what you want to get done in each study period, with a number of periods set aside for revision and for "catching up". Within your study period you must decide which subject to start with and how much time to allocate to each one. You should start with the most difficult so that you are working on this while you are fresh. You should end up with a subject that you find interesting. This will give you something more pleasant to look forward to. It will also be easier to work on this when you are getting tired, and it will leave you in a positive mood for your next study period. Assuming that all subjects are of equal importance, you should allot more time to the subjects you like least or find the most difficult. Occasionally you will have to spend extra time, outside of timetabled periods, when you are having a particularly tough time coping with a subject. This can mean going to the library at lunchtime or reading through the weekend. When you have dealt with the difficulty you will find that your improved concentration and sense of satisfaction was well worth the extra effort.

THE RIGHT ENVIRONMENT

Good concentration need not and does not solely depend on internal effort. The external environment also plays a part, for better or worse. You can increase the efficiency of your work by ensuring the following:

A Quiet Room
Ideally this would be a specially designed study, but few students have such a facility. Any room in which you are free from distractions such as T.V., stereo, noisy family members or friends, can be organized for study. It is best to habitually study in the same place, where everything is organized to suit and to provide a good work atmosphere. For those students who find it difficult to work alone for long periods of time, the library or study hall can provide a good study environment.

Adequate Lighting
A general room light as well as a desk lamp usually provides adequate lighting. The light should be evenly distributed and free from glare and shadows.

Adequate Heating and Ventilation

There should be enough heat to enable you to maintain body temperature comfortably (roughly in the range 60 - 70F), and an open window will ensure adequate ventilation.

Study Furniture

You should have a desk or table specifically for study, and a chair at the right height for the desk. Study is best done sitting in an erect position at a desk rather than in a easy chair. Some of the more straightforward reading can be done in an easy chair, but if the material is not very interesting you will be slower and more prone to sleepiness in this position. Your desk should always be tidy to facilitate ease of work, with nothing on it except what is needed for the study session. It is very helpful to have shelving above or beside the desk containing dictionaries and other reference books. A waste paper basket is a must.

A GOOD START

The greatest amount of lost study time occurs in putting off the actual start of real work. Everyone can identify with the person who sits at their desk, tidies it, doodles on the blank page, sharpens the pencils, rearranges the books, and feels that he/she has made a start. These activities are fine but they are not study and don't belong in the study period. The problem that most people have in getting started is in anticipating difficulty with the work, with concentration or with completing what has to be done. In other words they focus on the negative aspects of the task and ignore the rewarding aspects. Some feel that they need to "warm up" or get "into the mood". It takes practice to break these habits. Until you are starting your study sessions routinely on time you will need to provide yourself with external incentives for doing so. So each time you start your study on time you should have a treat organized for your break or for the end of the session. Tell people your starting time. Decide that you will have to make up any lost time either at the end of the session or in a free period.

The best way to settle down to effective study is to be active and to work quickly. If you are reading, take notes and make summaries as you go along (see the section on reading skills). If you are writing do so as quickly as possible. Don't allow yourself to stop between "bits" of work, e.g. on completing a maths problem or a paragraph of an essay. Focus on the final product. Remind yourself of the enjoyable break to come.

Length of Individual Study Units

Assume that your study period is from 6.00 p.m. to 10.00 p.m. The most effective way to divide your time would be as follows:

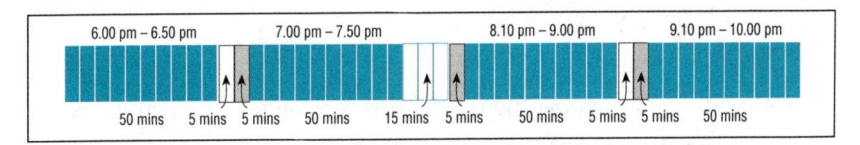

In each study hour you spend 50 minutes on study, take a five minute break, and spend five minutes revising what you did during the 50 minute period. After two study hours you take a 15 minute break and again five minutes revision of what you have done. The final period of the evening is reserved for your easiest task or the subject you like best.

If you find it difficult to concentrate on a particular subject, break the time down into two 20 minute units, rather than embarking on a full 50 minutes. You can use the extra minutes to look back over what you have done, to read ahead or to look at some more interesting aspect of the subject. The objective is to get work done, not just to spend 50 minutes at your desk!

Before taking any break, try to finish with something completed or have it in a form that will be reasonably easy to deal with when you get back. This will make it easier to return to. The ideal, of course, is when you "can't wait" to get back to what you were doing.

During the five minute breaks, get up from your desk, walk around, think about something different. During the 15 minute break leave the study room. This will be the time for a snack, to phone a friend, or chat with the family. On a particularly tough evening you may wish to devote some of this time to relaxation exercises (see Chapter 3).

DEALING WITH DISTRACTIONS

Distractions are of two types, internal and external. Both will occur while you study. Dealing with them effectively will (a) advance the quality of your study, and (b) prevent you from having to frequently over-run the allotted time for study (i.e. will give you more time for activities of your choice).

Internal Distractions
1. Worrying or thinking about other issues.
2. Day-dreaming.

The best way to handle the first is to write down your worry / plan / idea, and put it aside until the study period is over. Day-dreaming is a common enemy of study. The only way to deal with day-dreaming is to stop it immediately, as soon as you catch yourself at it. Use your thought-stopping technique (See Chapter 3), and tell yourself to "Stay relevant – do what has to be done". Repeat this as often as necessary.

External Distractions
The motto here should be "Only deal with emergencies". Otherwise get someone else to deal with the situation, or explain that you will deal with it, phone back, or whatever, at a certain time (i.e. at your longest break or when finished studying). This approach will take determination on your part as you may meet objections along the way. Being polite, although firm, will help in getting the necessary co-operation from everyone.

3. PERSISTENCE

A successful student is one who can stay with a subject, not only through a planned study period, but throughout an entire course. This ability depends on:

- Managing drops in motivation, and
- Meaningful, good quality learning

Managing Drops in Motivation

The reasons why we do things are rarely simple or singular. There are normally positive and negative reasons, and these shift and change in importance over time. Take study as an example. Some positive reasons to keep going would be the prospect of a good career, doing well in exams, getting a scholarship, pleasing parents and teachers, etc. Negative reasons might include avoiding criticism from parents or teachers, avoiding embarrassment in class, fear of rejection, fear of having to repeat a year, etc. But even students who have set goals and are strongly motivated generally, will face times when they feel like giving up. The reasons for this may be as simple as a mood change, or may result from a disappointing grade in an exam, a row with family or friends, a T.V. discussion on unemployment, etc.

Resisting the temptation to abandon study, whether temporarily within a study session or more long-term to pursue other activities, takes:

- Practice
- Use of private speech
- External supports

Practice

One of the most important methods of breaking old habits and developing new skills is frequent repetition, i.e. practice. Just doing something now and again, albeit successfully, is not sufficient. Under certain conditions (e.g. when tired, anxious, or suffering a minor illness) the new skill may break down unless it has been rehearsed and strengthened. This applies to the skill of being able to persist with work that is not intrinsically interesting or rewarding. You should see each temptation to give up as an opportunity to practice this skill, and go right back to work immediately. Each week you should seek a number of opportunities to study at times when you least feel like it (e.g. instead of watching the Sunday afternoon film, or while your friends are playing a card game). You will be rewarded for your effort not only by seeing work being done, but by the growing feeling of control over your life.

Use of Private Speech

Private speech plays a major role in dealing with distractions and temptations. You can talk yourself (mentally, not aloud!) through a situation that competes with your short, medium and long-term goals. The conscious use of self-statements (private speech) to counteract opposing demands might go something as follows:

> "Yes it would be super to go to the beach with the others, especially as they're bringing the surfboards. But is that what I really want? Think of what is most important – I will think again about my goals. I'll feel better tomorrow if I stick to my plan for today. I will organize something good for Sunday..."

External Supports

Arrange as many supports for persisting with your study as possible. These will include such things as the following:

> - Have items in your study room to spur you on (e.g. books, pictures, etc., relating to your career of interest)
> - Have family members and friends familiar with your work and your progress
> - Make use of all guidance and advisory services available in your school or college

In addition to such supports, an invaluable added support is participation in a Study Group.

FOUR HEADS ARE BETTER THAN ONE

Study Groups are common in American schools and universities, and are now beginning to be popular here also. Fellow students are a very powerful aid to learning, but their greatest value is in preparing for exams. The most successful study groups adhere to the following:

1. Choose people (3 - 4 in number) who are reasonably compatible.
2. Timetable their meetings (normally once or twice a week).
3. Commit themselves to attend (send apologies for absence).
4. Share out work amongst the members.
5. Set out a study agenda in advance.
6. Discipline themselves to a "work only" policy during the study session.

Working in a group not only helps with motivation and persistence, but is also a very effective learning and memory tool. You will understand and remember a lot more of what your friends have taught you, what you have debated with them, and what you have taught them, than you will from reading by yourself.

So if you are not a member of a Study Group, get one going!

4. MEANINGFUL, GOOD QUALITY LEARNING

Growth in knowledge and understanding, like other facets of human development, does not always proceed smoothly in set stages. Rather, it progresses at an irregular pace, at times rapidly, at times slowly, and at times seems to be "stuck" for a while. But in order to get the most benefit from your study, what you are learning should be meaningful and it should be learned in such a way that you can remember it when you need to use it. Basic requirements for good quality study are

- Knowing how to read textbooks, and
- Knowing how to get the most from classes/lectures

READING

Students, particularly at third level, are presented with long lists of books and articles to be read for each course, and they cannot possibly read each sentence in every recommended book. So you must select your reading material wisely, and approach each text in the most appropriate way. You must decide whether to skim over a book or whether to read it with close attention. One method that has proved very successful, and can be adapted to different types of reading requirements is known as SQ3R.

Survey	Read
Question	Recall
	Review

Survey

Instead of starting at the beginning of a book and reading through it, you should get a birds-eye view of the book, and know what it contains. A quick survey of the book will help you to read it with understanding and a critical appreciation. This involves:

1. Getting the following information:
   * The title and subtitle   * The author's name and qualifications
   * The date of publication.
2. Next, read the Preface/Forward/Introduction. This will tell you the purpose and scope of the book.
3. Then, the Table of Contents. This will inform you of the topics covered – essential for seeing what you will learn from the book or for making decisions about what to choose to read.
4. Leaf through the book from start to finish. Glance at tables and graphs, main headings and bold print. This gives a further general impression of the contents and the approach of the author to the subject.

Spend 10 - 20 minutes on your general survey.

Now you need to survey the first chapter. Each new chapter should be surveyed. Pay special attention to

- The first and last paragraph
- Headings
- Summaries

Question

Before you settle down to detailed reading of any text you should have a set of questions in mind that you wish to have answered by the book. This will give your reading a purpose and keep you active and alert. You will have formed questions during the survey stage, and you may have others of your own from previous knowledge of the area. The study group may have formed questions, or you may have been given set questions by your teacher.

Read

Reading is the third, not the first step in studying a book. You should read actively, i.e. always ask what the main idea is of the paragraph/section. Do not take notes or underline at this stage.

Read Again

This time take notes on the main ideas. Underline or highlight key points or phrases if the book belongs to you. Jot down any further questions that occur to you as you go along.

Recall

Reading and understanding a textbook does not mean that you will be able to recall the material later. Look at the following illustration:

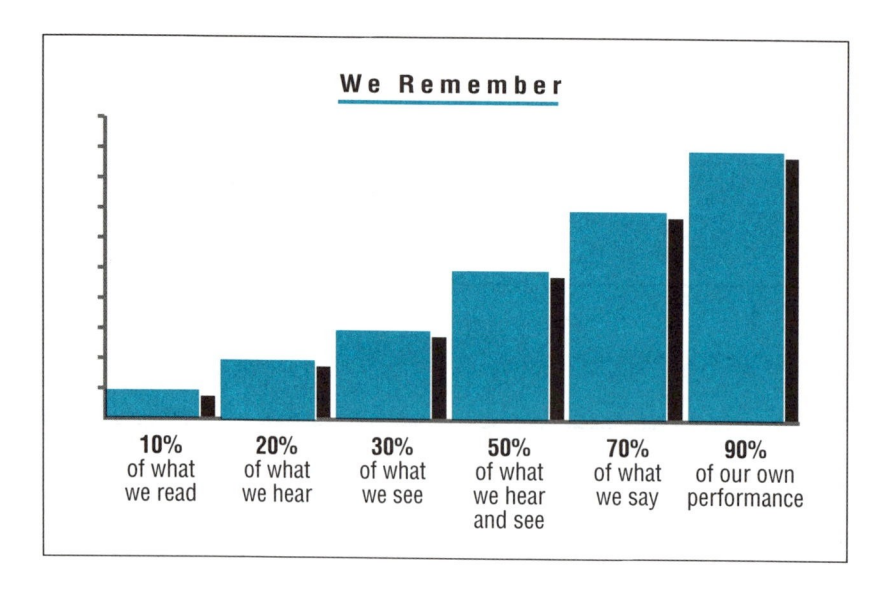

Only 10% of what you read will be retrievable later. Within seconds of putting down a book you will have forgotten 50% of what you have read, unless you have been active (questioning, looking for main ideas, taking notes), and unless you also make an attempt to recall what you have read. The best time to do this is at the end of each main section within the chapter. Recalling after each paragraph would interrupt the flow of your reading, and at the end of a chapter might risk your overlooking something you did not understand. So every time you see a new main heading, put your book down and recall the chapter until then. Write down the main points – this will help concentration and keep you active. A large proportion of your book study time should go on the recall stage – about half of the time.

Review

The final stage is checking how well you did on recall. Never assume that you have recalled correctly. The best way to do this is to do a quick survey of the section or chapter, then re-read it. Complete your review by filling in any gaps and correcting any errors in your recall.

The five steps of SQ3R have been tested by thousands of students and have been found to significantly increase the effectiveness of their study. It is flexible, and can be modified to suit different needs, e.g. it can also be adapted to classes/lectures.

GETTING THE MOST FROM YOUR CLASS/LECTURE

Some classes/lectures can be very exciting and challenging, others can be downright boring. Teachers come in all varieties, and unless you have chosen a subject on the basis of who teaches it (a most unwise thing to do) then it is pretty much "pot luck" how good your teacher will be at presenting his/her material. But regardless of their style of presentation, all teachers want their students to succeed, and all are anxious to help in any way possible for them to do so.

What you get from your education is largely up to you. If you see it as your responsibility you will want to get the most from all of your classes/lectures. In order to do so you will need to

- Take an active role
- Develop good note-taking skills

Be Active In Class

As already mentioned, the SQ3R system can be adapted to the class or lecture:

Survey: Only possible if your teacher outlines what is to be covered during the class period. But reading ahead will give you an idea of topics to come. It is worth asking for a plan of the course in advance.

Question: Listen questioningly as the teacher speaks. Ask him/her to clarify points you don't understand or to repeat what you have missed. Ask questions of your own (sometimes these are best asked after the class has ended).

Read: Listening serves the same function at a class or lecture.

Recall: This is essential and best done as soon as possible after the class is over.

Review: Use your study group or other students to verify what you have recalled. Your lecturer will be happy to help when you are stuck.

As well as asking questions, always try to join in at class discussions. You will remember more of what you have contributed than what has been said by anyone else. If you find it very difficult to speak in class, have a word with your school/college counsellor who will advise you on how to overcome this problem. But you will be surprised how much easier it becomes after a little practice.

Note-Taking

Poor note-taking is a common cause of failure for students. Notes are an extremely important part of learning. They

- Help you to keep active (thus aiding concentration)
- Help you to understand and memorize the course material
- Put the course material in your own familiar words and style
- Form the basis for effective revision

Good note-taking is a skill which takes practice to develop. In order to get the most benefit from your note-taking you should do the following:

1. Have a sturdy notebook for each subject, and keep notes on particular topics together. A loose-leaf binder is a good choice for this.
2. Take notes in outline form and in your own words – not verbatim. Write down the main points, threading them together to show the overall theme of the lecture. Use main headings and subheadings. Underline key points or phrases. Don't write large blocks of text.
3. Write down anything that "grabs" your attention – a catch phrase, joke (relevant of course), interesting point or quotation. This will bring back the flavour of the lecture later, making recall easier.
4. As soon as possible after your class/lecture recall as much of it as you can with the aid of your notes. Reconstruct the lecture, filling in the gaps in your notes as you go along.
5. Identify anything that you don't fully understand. Make sure that you sort this out, either by yourself, in your study group or by asking your teacher.
6. Re-write your notes, this time in a form that you will understand at a glance no matter how long it will be before you go back to revise.

Do this by using headings, subheadings, numbering of points, and indenting. Put extra details or explanations in brackets. Underline or highlight key phrases, concepts or terminology. Use diagrams and drawings where possible.

7. Label and date your write-up of each class/lecture.

This method will help you to improve your note-taking and provide you with a set of notes that will enhance your understanding and appreciation of the subject, and greatly increase your chances of good revision right up to exam time.

2. TIME MANAGEMENT

5. USING PRECIOUS TIME WISELY

It is 7.30 p.m. Harry switches off the TV and heads for his room to start his evening's study. He had intended starting at 7.00 p.m. but Harry felt that the comedy programme was too funny to be missed. He sits at his desk and searches through the books in his briefcase. He decides to start with the poetry as he finds this fairly easy. The maths problems have to be done for tomorrow but he will get to these later. He spends 30 minutes on the poetry. This is taking longer than he expected. He goes for an apple. He gazes out the window as he munches the apple, and then sits down again. A further 20 minutes of poetry and he puts it away for the night. Now for the maths. He takes out the books, pencil-case, calculator. He didn't really understand what was done in class today so he will have to read over Chapter 5 again. He pushes the maths books to one side and switches to French. He hears the telephone – could it be Donna? He wonders if she is going to the match after school tomorrow. He decides to give her a ring. Fifteen minutes later he is back at his desk. He finds it hard to concentrate on the French because Donna told him that she hates rugby. He reads through two chapters, underlining the main points as he goes. Now for the maths. He feels hungry. A snack would help. There is an argument going on in the kitchen about whether to invite the Kellys to the barbecue on Saturday. Harry gets involved. It is now 9.30 p.m. and Harry has glanced over Chapter 5. He begins to panic about the maths problems. He turns on the stereo as background music and tries to settle down. By 10.15 p.m. he has two done and three to go. His mother comes into the room and Harry complains that he can't possibly get everything done. When asked what he has been doing all night Harry answers with genuine sincerity – "Studying of course!".

Harry is a rather extreme case of poor study skills. However, most students could identify with him. Everyone has difficulty with concentration at times, and everyone is tempted to put off what they do not like.

What distinguishes the good student from the poor student, more than any other factor, is the use of plans and timetables. Without them even the most intelligent student will stagger between bouts of work, the frittering away of time, frantic catching up, frustration and disappointment. By using plans and timetables you will find that

- You normally get assignments finished on time
- You work in a more relaxed and confident way
- The quality of your work improves
- You have more free time to do other things

But remember, making out a timetable is relatively easy. Sticking to it takes determination and effort. We have looked at the importance of motivation and persistence. The rest of this chapter will show you how to plan your time effectively.

Let's take Harry's situation as an example of how to build an effective plan.

Harry has four days of classes from 9 a.m. until 4 p.m., and on Wednesdays he has classes from 9 a.m. until 1 p.m. He studies piano on Mondays from 4.30 until 5.30 p.m. He likes to play squash and to go to soccer and rugby matches. He has a girlfriend and they usually go out together or with other friends each week. Harry needs

1. A Master Plan (Wallchart)
2. A Weekly Timetable

The Master Plan

This is your plan for the entire year. On this you can see at a glance how your year is mapped out. It should have two sections

1. A small section for the academic year, September to June, with space under each month for writing in important dates. Here you write in exam dates – noting down the subject and whether it is a class exam, end-of-term or final exam. Write in due dates for assignments – essays, projects, etc. This will be updated as you move through the year. Write in any events that will take you from your classes or interrupt your routine – field trips, etc.

2. A larger section for your study plan on a weekly basis. On this you put in all set classes/lectures, tutorials, practicals, etc. You also put in any other fixed events – music lessons, sports training sessions, etc.

   Now you must decide the amount of time you will devote to private study in a week, and the best time to do the study. The private study periods are then written in on the study plan.

How Much Study?

There is no fixed rule about how much study is right for everyone. And there will be times, e.g. toward the end of the year, when the amount of study will increase, regardless of your initial plan. But in order to get through the exam system successfully you must be prepared to give very generous amounts of time to private study, i.e. a minimum of 25 hours per week outside of set class or lecture periods. Less than this would be inadequate, and more than a total of 60 hours' study including classes/lectures could lessen the efficiency of your work and interfere with other important aspects of your life (socializing, leisure reading, sports, etc.).

Allow one free day each week. This would normally be Sunday.

Allow one other free evening, and one other free half day.

When To Study

A number of study hours can usually be found between lectures by third level students, but for all students the greater part of private study is done in the evenings between 6.00 p.m. and 11.00 p.m. A number of students study later – sometimes into the early hours, but this is certainly not a good idea. Your ability to process information is lower at that stage, and you will find it hard to be alert at morning classes when much of the more important instruction is given. You should finish studying an hour before you go to bed, to allow time to relax and mix with the family. So if you normally go to bed at 11.00 p.m. try to have your study finished by 10.00 p.m. Occasionally, when completing a big task, work later than this. But do not let this become a habit.

The Weekly Timetable

This is your flexible guide to the week ahead. It details for you what exactly you will work at during any one study period. Each week's timetable is made out fresh at the beginning of the week, and is guided by

- Routine homework
- Upcoming events on the Master Plan – assignments due, class exam, etc.
- Particular difficulties in any subject needing more time

You will also need to provide periods for REVISION, for READING AHEAD and for CATCHING UP (this is a rag-bag period when you do the work that was timetabled but didn't get finished).

The Weekly Timetable can be photocopied.
Use this to plan each week's study.

Harry has pinned up his Master Plan. He has also filled in his Weekly Timetable for the coming week.

Harry's timetable becomes his number one commitment. Only an emergency can deflect him from his plan. In time it will be a natural part of his life. He is now well on his way to becoming a very successful student.

Weekly Timetable

Name ....

Week Beginning ....

	M	T	W	Th.	F	S	S
10 -11							
11-12							
12 - 1							
1 - 2							
2 - 3							
3 - 4							
4 - 5							
5 - 6							
6 - 7							
7 - 8							
8 - 9							
9 - 10							

3. COPING SKILLS

6. HOW TO BE A GOOD PROBLEM-SOLVER

Think about your life right now. How many problems have you? Jot them all down on a sheet of paper.

Are there five? Ten? More? Now see how many of them involve other people – parents, friends, teachers, boy/girlfriend.

How do you feel about each problem? How confident are you that you can solve it?

Problems are very much a part of every student's life, and most manage to work them out alright and to survive the "disasters". However, knowing how to approach a problem, and what steps to take to achieve the best outcome, will not only give you confidence, but will also free you from a lot of worry that can interfere with your studies and with other important areas of your life.

Are You A Good Problem-Solver?

Answer the following questions about how you deal with your own problems. Then compare your answers with those given by good problem-solvers.

1. When you have a problem with another person do you usually feel you will be able to solve it effectively? YES ❏ NO ❏

2. If you try to make things better between yourself and someone else and the situation does not improve, do you usually then stop trying? YES ❏ NO ❏

3. Can you normally disagree with someone without getting upset? YES ❏ NO ❏

4. When you feel upset do you act without thinking clearly? YES ❏ NO ❏

5. When you have a problem with another person do you usually try to avoid doing anything about it if possible?   YES ❏   NO ❏

6. Do you usually think out the consequences before acting on a problem?   YES ❏   NO ❏

7. Do you usually try to get a problem over with immediately?   YES ❏   NO ❏

8. If the other person gets upset or angry, do you usually get upset or angry yourself?   YES ❏   NO ❏

9. Do you usually find out exactly what the other person wants by asking him/her?   YES ❏   NO ❏

10. When you act on a problem do you often end up regretting what you have done?   YES ❏   NO ❏

11. Do you usually consider more than one way of solving a problem before trying anything?   YES ❏   NO ❏

12. Are your feelings often very hurt by other people?   YES ❏   NO ❏

13. Do you usually explain yourself well?   YES ❏   NO ❏

14. Do you think that your problems are much the same as other people's?   YES ❏   NO ❏

15. Is there only one good solution to every problem?   YES ❏   NO ❏

The Answers of Good Problem-Solvers

1. Yes	2. No	3. Yes	4. No	5. No	6. Yes
7. No	8. No	9. Yes	10. No	11. Yes	12. No
13. Yes	14. Yes	15. No			

How many of these answers did you have?

You can learn to become an effective problem-solver. But you will have to practise the skills involved.

As an example we will take George's problem. George's family has moved house and he has had to change to a new school. He has another year of school to go and now he has no friends. On his first day he feels tense and awkward. He would like to make friends, but he is a bit shy and finds it hard to break in to the social groups. None of the other boys pay much attention to him. But George is a good problem-solver. He knows the five steps involved in getting the best outcome for any problem. These are set out in the following table.

THE FIVE STAGES OF EFFECTIVE PROBLEM-SOLVING

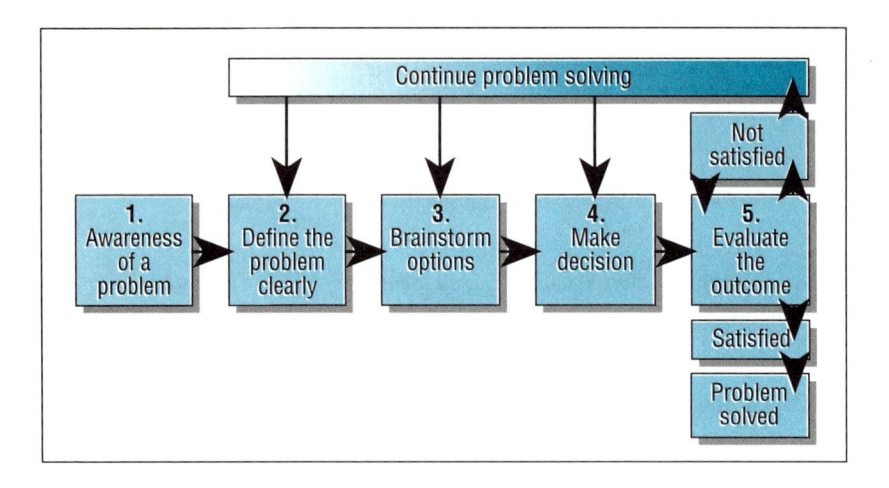

1. General Approach to a Problem

Recognition *of Problems as they Arise*

No matter how small or big a problem is, you should try to recognize it as early as possible so that you can start working on it before it has a chance to grow any bigger. We recognize that we have a problem when

> OUR EMOTIONS TELL US SOMETHING IS WRONG
> AND THERE IS A DISCREPANCY BETWEEN WHAT
> IS HAPPENING AND WHAT WE WOULD LIKE TO
> HAPPEN

Acceptance *of Problems as Normal*

It is normal to have problems. It is not possible to live life without them. So you must expect to be continually faced with problems - each day will call on your problem-solving skills.

Control *the Urge To Act Too Quickly or To Avoid the Problem*

Two mistakes that are commonly made when problems first arise, particularly when we feel upset, are either to act impulsively, or to hope that the problem will just go away and to avoid doing anything about it. Either of these reactions is likely to make a problem worse.

So, the first step is to acknowledge that a problem exists as soon as it arises, see it as a normal part of your life, and prepare yourself to work on it in a planned way.

2. Define the Problem Clearly

Very often we have only a vague idea of what the problem is that is making us feel bad, e.g. George could have just said to himself: "They're not very friendly....I'm not going to be happy here". But defining a problem clearly is a very important stage.

If you do this well the remaining problem-solving steps are made a lot easier. This involves the following:

Set out *the discrepancy between what is happening and what you would like – in specific, concrete terms.*

> George – "I have no friends at my new school. I would like three or four friends".
> His GOAL is to make three or four friends.

Get Information

What do you need to know to help you to solve the problem? Set out all the relevant facts.

George needs to find out things like: who lives near him ... what sports are on and when ... what clubs/societies he can join ... what the other boys do during free periods/lunchtime... whether anyone shares his interest in model railways and airplanes... whether they go to parties ... etc.

You get the information you need mainly by – LOOKING, LISTENING and ASKING QUESTIONS. If you appear friendly and seem interested this stage will be a lot easier.

Identify Obstacles

What are the obstacles that are making the situation difficult?

> For George – the other students have made their friends already... He is shy – he hates approaching people he doesn't know... The boys don't seem interested in him ...
>
> He doesn't have anyone to help him to get started ...

George knows that it is quite normal to feel shy and awkward initially, so he won't let this stand in his way. He will work particularly hard at spotting at least two boys who are easy to approach and sit near them, ask them for help with timetables, etc., for a while.

So you have defined the problem clearly, got your information and dealt with any obstacles. You are now ready for the next step.

3. Finding Options

You should find as many options as possible for dealing with any one problem. This way you won't get disheartened when something doesn't work out – instead you go on to your next option. The best method for coming up with a lot of different alternatives is called **BRAINSTORMING**.

The rules of Brainstorming are:

> Criticism is ruled out
> "Free-wheeling" is welcomed
> Quantity is wanted
> Combine and improve ideas as you go along

Get a large sheet of paper and a pencil and put down all the ideas that occur to you. As long as they are related to your goal anything goes. Wild ideas – free-wheeling – helps to loosen up your thinking. There is no such thing as a "bad" idea at this stage. You will sort them out later.

George has just started his list. Let's have a look –

Join the soccer team ... throw a video party ... invite one or two to fly my plane with me ... do nothing ... pick a fight to get attention ... bring in some of my tapes or books ... ask Bill how the library works – he looks easy-going .... visit the counsellor ... stay off school for a while ... leave school ... ride home with Jim and Ronan – they live nearby.

If you follow the four brainstorming rules you will produce a lot of ideas to choose from.

4. Decision Making

The important thing here is going through the steps in making a decision, not whether the decision itself turns out to be the one that solves the problem. Once you know the steps to take you can always repeat the process if you are not happy with the outcome. So you have made a good decision if you have gone through the right steps in making it, whether or not the decision you make actually turns out to be the best one.

You now choose from the list those options most likely to be useful in reaching your goal. But first you will have to cross out any that would be likely to have highly negative consequences.

George crosses out: "do nothing" (the problem will remain or get worse) ... "pick a fight" (enemies straight away, get on wrong side of teachers) ... "stay off school" (harder to face the problem a second time) ... "leave school" (miss the chance of getting the Leaving Certificate and need this to do the marketing course, trouble with parents).

The options that are left are now looked at individually. For each one, all the advantages and disadvantages are set out. When first practicing these skills, and with any important problem, writing out the various steps helps to keep your thinking clear. Use a large sheet of paper, and draw a line down the centre. For each option, list all of the advantages on one side and the disadvantages on the other – these are the consequences.

When all options have been analysed as to their consequences, they are all then ranked as to the best 'payoff'. You now know which one you consider the best, next best and so on.

George's highest ranked options are:

1. Ride home with Jim and Ronan.
2. Join the soccer team.
3. Stay at school for lunch instead of going home.
4. Visit the counsellor.

So you have decided what to do about your problem. Now you must act on your decision. Choose the highest ranked option (or more if a number of options should be gone ahead with), and carry it out to the best of your ability.

5. Evaluation

The purpose of going through all the problem-solving steps was to maximise your chances that the chosen course of action would have a favourable outcome. The final stage – evaluation – is designed to assess the actual outcome. Without this step you might carry on with a course of action that isn't very helpful, instead of attempting to find out where the trouble is and correcting it.

Consider carefully the GOAL and the OUTCOME, and decide whether you feel reasonably satisfied with how they match. Don't look for a perfect outcome – this rarely happens.

> George has carried out options 1 and 2. He now looks
> again at his goal – to make three or four friends. He looks
> at the outcome. How do they match? He quite enjoys
> riding home with Ronan, and Ronan has already asked to
> see his model airplane. He finds Jim a bit too serious. The
> soccer is good, but unfortunately the main training session
> is on Saturday morning, when George works for two hours
> at the supermarket – he will never make the team this way.

George is not yet satisfied. Being a good problem-solver, he doesn't get disheartened. He knows what to do – he decides which step of the problem-solving process to return to. He sees that he has a new problem – the Saturday morning clash. He will go back to the first stage for this one. In addition he decides to implement his next option on his list, staying at school for lunch. He will continue in this planned way until he feels that he has, or soon will have made some new friends.

It is very important to be ready to resume the problem-solving process when you are not satisfied with the outcome. This "recycling" of problems is the norm rather than the exception. So, depending on what you feel needs to be done, you will go back again, e.g.

A different problem has emerged	–	return to stage 1
Further information is needed	–	return to stage 2
Additional options need to be found	–	return to stage 3
A different option needs to be selected	–	return to stage 4

When you believe that the outcome is reasonably satisfactory – STOP - - - - - PROBLEM SOLVED - - - - - WELL DONE!

7. CONTROLLING STRESS AND REDUCING ANXIETY

Stress is part of normal life. It is as much a part of everyone's life as hunger, thirst, curiosity, love. Most people think of stress in a very negative way, as something to be avoided, as something harmful. Stress cannot be avoided, and its effects are harmful only when it is badly handled. The proper handling of stress produces growth and enhances the quality of life.

Stress refers to a state that the body adopts in order to protect itself against a challenging, demanding or threatening situation. The body prepares itself to either fight the challenge or to flee the situation, sometimes referred to as the "fight or flight" reaction which evolved at a time when our environment was a truly dangerous place to inhabit. The heart rate increases, muscles tense, breathing becomes faster, the pupils dilate, and blood vessels close to the surface of the skin constrict. We experience these changes as stress or nervous tension. The changes tend to be quite similar even when triggered by very different stressors. A stressor is any event or thought that triggers the stress reaction. For many students, stressors include such experiences as starting in a new school or college, rushing for the school bus at the last minute, setting out for the first summer job, going to the dentist, or examinations. But as well as threatening or frustrating events, stressors can also include challenging or demanding events, e.g. going on your first date, competing in a race, even setting out on a foreign holiday. Emotionally we view these changes in a negative way when we interpret the stressor as a threat (e.g. the dentist or the exam), or in a less negative way when we see the event as challenging or very exciting (e.g. the race or the first date).

It was once believed that only external events caused stress, but we now know that this is not the case. Stress is not caused by a particular situation as such. It is caused by how we interpret or view the situation. What is stressful for one person may not be at all stressful for another.

Consider two people, Ann and Tom, going to the same party. Ann is looking forward to the party, to meeting her friends, and to the possibility of finding a new boyfriend. Tom, however, is imagining himself standing alone in the room, being ignored, and finding it impossible to think of things to say. He wonders whether he will go at all. On the way to the party Ann feels slightly "wound up" but pays no attention to the bodily sensations as her thoughts are on the good time to come. Tom, on the other hand, is focussed in on his upset stomach, his tight chest and sweaty palms. These unpleasant sensations are used by Tom to further convince himself that he will be miserable at the party. His negative thoughts in turn increase his level of tension. This cycle of negative thinking and increasing tension will leave Tom feeling very anxious, and when he arrives at the party he will find it difficult to settle down and enjoy himself. Ann, however, is likely to settle in easily and have a good time.

The actual situation is the same for both people. It's their view of the situation that is different, in one case causing stress/anxiety, and in the other causing no significant stress at all. *Your mind tells your body whether a situation is threatening and your body responds accordingly.*

There are also times when you feel tense and anxious but don't really know why. Often this will pass without needing any particular attention paid to it. A brisk walk, a chat with a friend, a good TV programme – doing something you enjoy will usually leave you feeling much better.

However, if you still have an uncomfortable level of tension/anxiety, then you are probably engaging in automatic negative thinking, without being aware of it. There are many situations which we fear or worry about, but because we either developed the fear in early childhood or encounter the situation so often, we are no longer aware of what it is we are saying to ourselves about it. We are only aware of the bodily sensations. The thoughts, or images (we think in pictures too), occur automatically and so fast that we don't "catch" them or process them consciously. For example, if you start crossing a street and a truck is speeding toward you, you don't stop to think "This truck is going very fast. It could kill me. I had better prepare myself to get out of its way!". Instead, your muscles tense, your heart-rate increases and you jump back onto the footpath. Your thoughts about the danger were so automatic and fast that you acted almost instantaneously. In this example the danger was real. However, there are many situations that trigger a stress/anxiety response that are not actually dangerous or threatening, but we have learned to fear them. And in between are those situations that most people find stressful, e.g. exams. Whether you cope well or not so well with these situations depends to a large extent on how effective you are at stress management.

The following figure illustrates the difference in the course of anxiety when you use effective anxiety management and when there is no deliberate attempt at managing it.

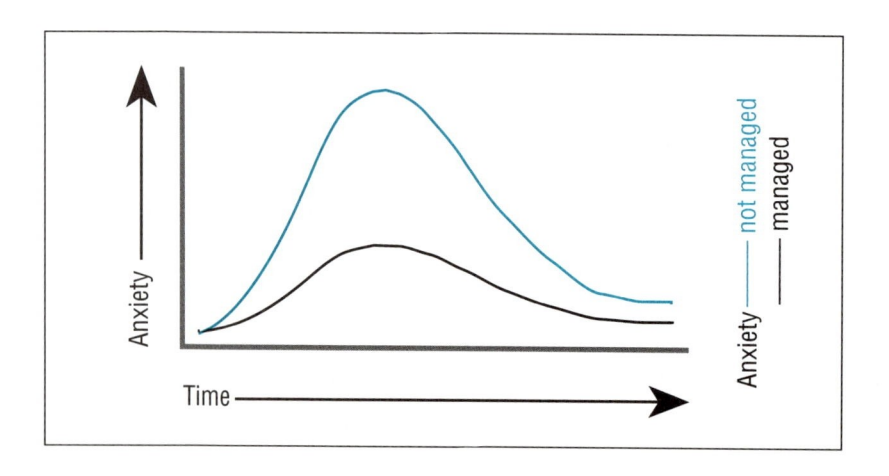

The rest of this chapter will provide you with the information you need to be able to manage stress effectively and reduce anxiety.

EFFECTIVE MANAGEMENT OF STRESSFUL EVENTS

While ability/intelligence is certainly one component for academic success, it is by no means the only one. High intelligence is not sufficient in itself for success. The majority of students are average, some are very bright and some are below average. Whichever category you fit into you will ensure that you achieve your best possible exam results by managing the stressful events of school/college life in an effective way. This will help you to feel in control and to feel confident about the future.

It is not difficult to be an effective stress manager, but there are skills that you will have to learn. Like learning any other skill, such as swimming or driving, it takes practice to be able to do it well. So you must be prepared to practice your new skills and apply them at every opportunity. Then when you get into the most stressful of all situations – the exam – you are well prepared and in control.

The most important skills that you will need to be able to manage stress and anxiety effectively are:

* Early detection of the stress response
* Controlling negative, irrational thoughts
* Relaxation techniques
* Problem Solving skills
* Time Management skills
* Effective Study skills

Separate chapters are devoted to Relaxation, Problem Solving, Time Management and Study Skills. However, the successful student uses all of these skills in an integrated way, applying them naturally to the everyday hassles and stresses of school or college life.

Consider Jean who has a Biology test in two weeks time. She has been letting her Biology studies fall behind and has not even started her revision yet. She has an essay to hand in by the following week on "Germany – before and after the Wall". She has been asked to go to a weekend club outing by a boy she has fancied for a long time. Jean is sitting in her room surrounded by books but cannot get started on anything. Her body feels tense. Her mouth is dry. She feels a "lump" in her throat. She thinks "I'll never get all this done in time. I haven't a clue about Germany. I'm going to fail Biology. Tony will think I'm not interested in him if I don't go on the weekend". She begins to feel helpless and panicky. What can Jean do?

STEP 1. LISTEN TO YOUR BODY –
DETECT THE EARLY SIGNS OF STRESS

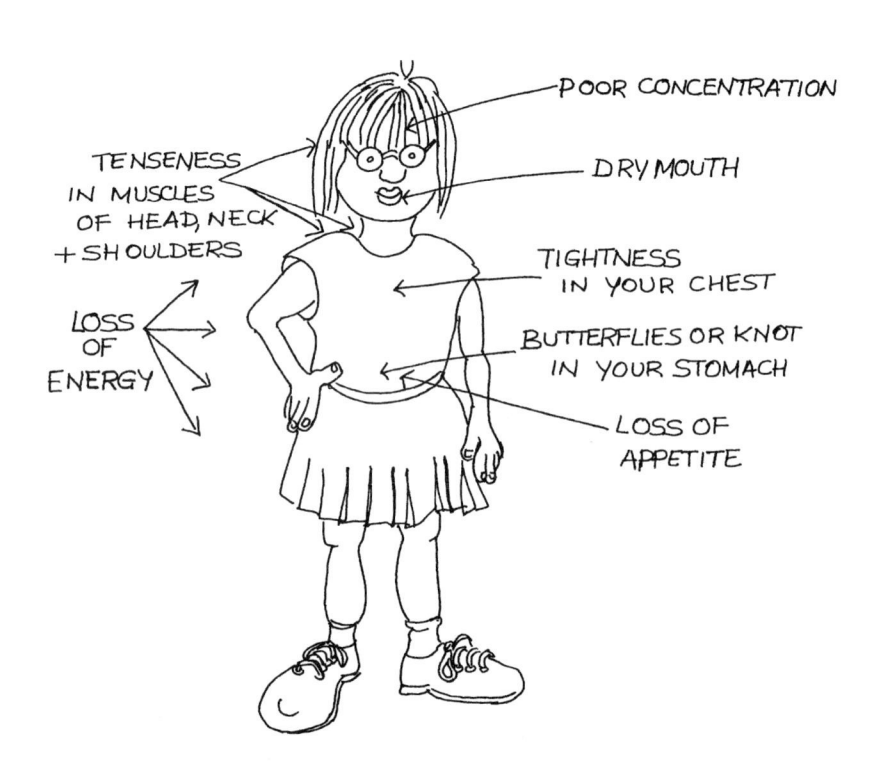

Listen to your body. It will tell you that something is wrong. You must learn to tune in to the early warning signs – such as:

- Butterflies or a knot in your stomach
- Tightness in your chest
- Changes in breathing
- Tenseness in the muscles of the head, neck, shoulders
- Dry mouth
- Poor concentration
- Loss of energy
- Loss of appetite

Take note of any such changes. They are important. They are your cue to look further into what is happening.

You should first rule out any purely physiological reasons for the discomfort, e.g. caffeine (palpitations), strenuous physical activity, e.g. running with a heavy bag (fast heartbeat, sweating), pre-menstrual tension, oncoming 'flu, etc. If this check does not provide a possible reason for the increase in tension/anxiety, then you proceed with the following steps to deal with it.

STEP 2 DEEP MUSCULAR RELAXATION

Section 8 shows you how to train yourself in simple, effective relaxation techniques. When you detect tension in your body you should do the exercises to relax all of your muscles first, and then focus on the main area of tension, e.g. chest, stomach. Check your breathing – is it deep and regular? Spend 2-3 minutes on controlled breathing, focussing your thoughts on the word R - E - L - A - X as you breathe out slowly.

STEP 3   LISTEN TO YOUR THOUGHTS – DETECT THE NEGATIVE SELF-TALK

What is it that you are telling yourself? Try to catch the negative self-statements that are in your mind – guess if you have to. These negative automatic thoughts are the real cause of your tension and anxiety, not the situation itself. Once you have figured out what it is that you are saying to yourself, then you must come up with some rational, positive answers for each negative thought. You may not quite believe these rational answers at first, but at least you are then aware of them and everything in your mind is not "all worry". If you can see some possibilities for positive action, some reasons why the situation might not be so bad, then you are much less likely to panic or to get too upset.

A good idea when you are first practicing this skill is to draw a line down the centre of a page. Jot down all the negative thoughts on one side, and the rational answers on the other.

Let's look at Jean's attempt.

JEAN'S NEGATIVE THOUGHTS	JEAN'S RATIONAL RESPONSES
I have too much to do	I have a lot to do... but I probably have more done than some others... It always seems like a lot more before a plan is made... My first step is to make out a plan....

I haven't enough time	I have a certain amount of time… If I use each hour well I can get a lot done… Stop fussing… Make out a timetable….
I haven't a clue about Germany	That's not quite true… I could at least write about the day the news broke…. I can ask Mom for information, she took an interest… There should be lots of good newspaper articles…
I'll fail Biology	It's very hard to fail… Even if I do it's not the end of everything… I don't have to know it all… I will pick 3 or 4 topics…
Tony will think I'm not interested	I can explain to him… Maybe he would help with the German essay… I'll ask him to go for a game of tennis when the exams are over….

Now Jean has made a good start to reducing her anxiety. She will soon notice her body responding – she will start to feel more calm, she will feel her energy coming back, and this in turn will help her to think more positively and to feel more optimistic.

SOME FURTHER USEFUL TECHNIQUES

Thought Stopping – Get a Rubber Band

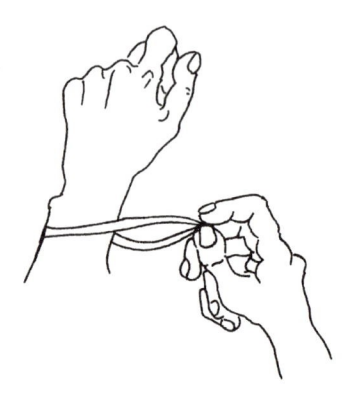

Sometimes, despite our best efforts, negative thoughts creep back and nag relentlessly. This is called "rumination". Rumination gets in the way of pursuing a positive course of action. This is where the "thought-stopping" technique comes in handy.

Once you have decided that a thought is negative and self-defeating, and you have worked out a rational response to it, you then deliberately prevent that thought from getting a further foothold. This is how you do it.

Equip yourself with a rubber band and put it on your wrist (the one you don't write with). It should be loose. At the first sign of the thought returning snap the band with the fingers of the other hand (don't hurt yourself – it's just to focus your attention). At the same time mentally shout STOP to yourself. This will cut off the thought and you can then deliberately think of the rational response (use a coping card if necessary - see below) or distract yourself with other thoughts or activities.

If the thought filters back you may have to do this a number of times. However, each time you stop the thought in this way you will weaken it, and it will eventually fade away.

Jean needs to use thought-stopping. She has done her relaxation and has managed to change her thinking about the essay and the test. Her tension level is reducing and she sets out to make out her timetable. However, she finds that she is haunted by the image of Tony having a great time with another girl on the club outing. She has worked on these thoughts but the image filters back. She goes for her elastic band and is now ready to pounce on the thought at the first sign of it reappearing. She may have to do this a number of times before she has control over the rumination.

Thought-stopping is particularly useful for dealing with the stress of exams, as this is a time when rumination on failure and a variety of possible "disasters" can be particularly bothersome.

Coping Cards – Ready-Made Help At Hand

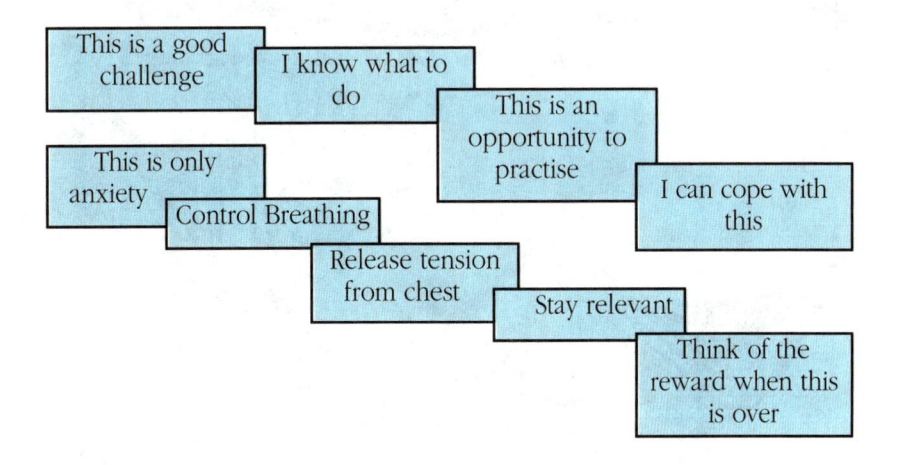

A useful method of organizing a good store of positive coping responses is to have a set of Coping Cards. These are small cards (4" x 2") on which you write a different coping self-statement or instruction . These are your own statements and everyone's set of cards will contain something different. Make out 15 - 20 well in advance of your exam.

Some Examples

> - I know how to control anxiety
> - Anxiety is harmless – it's just uncomfortable
> - Stay relevant – focus on the job to be done
> - Deep breathing – I - N – R - E - L - A - X
> - Don't mind about anyone else
> - I have done my best. Now for the rewards

You should carry these around with you. Read through them again and again. Imagine yourself facing an exam – then take out your cards and go through them slowly. On the morning or afternoon of the actual exam the coping cards can come in handy if your anxiety is too high to allow you to analyse your thinking. If you panic at the exam you can call on these coping statements as you will then know them off by heart.

8. DEEP MUSCULAR RELAXATION

Why do relaxation exercises?

> - Stress and anxiety are related to muscular tension
> - When you reduce muscular tension, you also reduce stress and anxiety
> - Deep muscular relaxation is a powerful way to train yourself to recognize the difference between tension and relaxation. With enough practice you will be able to detect tension and release it anywhere at any time

Deep muscular relaxation has been shown to be effective for:

> - Insomnia
> - Essential hypertension
> - Tension headache
> - Subjective reports of anxiety
> - Development of a calmer attitude

Deep muscular relaxation works, but you must be prepared to devote at least 15 minutes each day to it. The mistake that most people make is to rush through the relaxation procedure. As with any skill, the more you practise the more skilled you will become.

Deep muscular relaxation involves a series of exercises during which you tense (contract) and then release (relax) selected muscles. Before embarking on the exercises you should take note of the following:

1. If you have any problems with your muscles, e.g. weak or damaged muscles, or any bone problems, avoid that particular muscle group until you get advice from your doctor.
2. There is a difference between the desired muscle "tension" and undesirable muscle "strain". Tension is felt by a tightened, somewhat uncomfortable sensation in the muscles being tensed. You will know

that you have strained a muscle if you feel any pain in the muscle or the joints around it, or if it begins to tremble uncontrollably. These are signs to use less tension, or simply avoid that exercise.

3. Do not hold your breath while tensing muscles. Instead, breathe normally, or inhale while tensing and exhale while relaxing the muscles.

4. The right environment is very important for relaxation. You should do the exercises in quiet, comfortable surroundings, darkened if possible. Wear loose clothing. Remove contact lenses or glasses. Remove shoes if you like. Support your body with a comfortable chair. You can also do the exercises lying in bed at night if you have difficulty in falling asleep.

5. You may wish to tape the instructions on a cassette for yourself. This way you can give your entire attention to the sensations in your body rather than having to think of the next exercise.

6. When you tense a muscle group, hold the tension for about five seconds before relaxing. Pause for 5-10 seconds between exercises.

7. The entire procedure lasts for 15-20 minutes should you wish to relax your entire body. The time may be less if you choose to relax only a few muscle groups.

8. Don't worry about how well you are relaxing. If your mind wanders, gently return to the exercises by thinking the words

"C-A-L-M —— S-E-R-E-N-E"

BEGIN

You are now ready to relax the major muscle groups in your body in order to achieve a state of total relaxation.

Firstly, settle back into the chair in a very comfortable position. Close your eyes. Focus your attention on your breathing. The breath is the body's metronome. Become aware of the rhythm of your breathing – the air coming in through your nostrils and down into your lungs, expanding your chest and stomach – the chest and stomach receding as the air leaves your lungs. Focus on your breathing for about 30 seconds.

Chest

Begin with your chest. Take a very, very deep breath, while you bring your shoulders back. Breathe in all the air around you. Hold it for about five seconds .... and relax .... exhale all the air from your lungs. Resume your normal breathing. Did you notice the difference between the tension in your chest when you inhaled and the relaxation when you exhaled? Keep this in mind as you repeat the exercise. Again ... deep breath, shoulders back .... hold it ... and relax.

Now focus on the feeling of relaxation all through the chest area.

Lower Legs

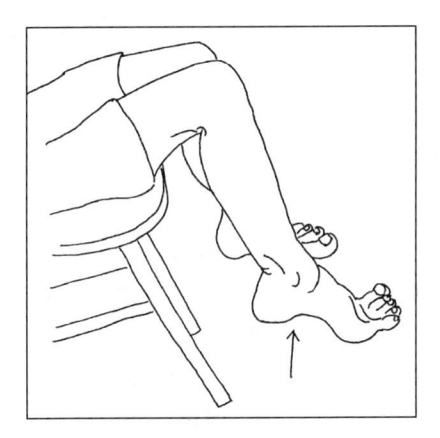 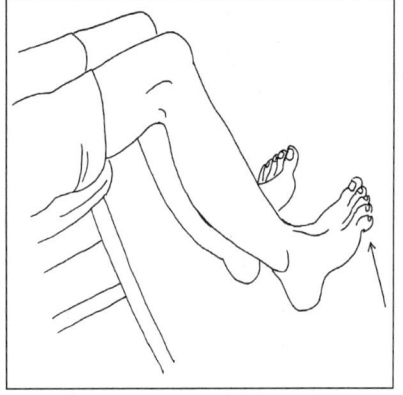

Now to the lower legs and the muscles in the calf. Firstly, place both your feet flat on the floor. Now, leaving your toes flat on the floor, raise both your heels at the same time as high as they will go. Raise them both very high ... hold it ... focus on the tension in the muscles ... and relax – let them fall gently back to the floor. Focus on the sensation as the muscles loosen and relax. Repeat this once more.

Now to work the opposite set of muscles, leave your heels flat on the floor. Point both sets of your toes very, very high. Point them as high as you can toward the ceiling ... Hold it... Relax.

Repeat this exercise – raising the toes even higher this time. Hold it, and relax.

Focus on the warmth, tingling, or heaviness in your lower legs.

This tells you that the muscles are relaxed. Let them become looser, heavier, and heavier.

Thighs and Stomach

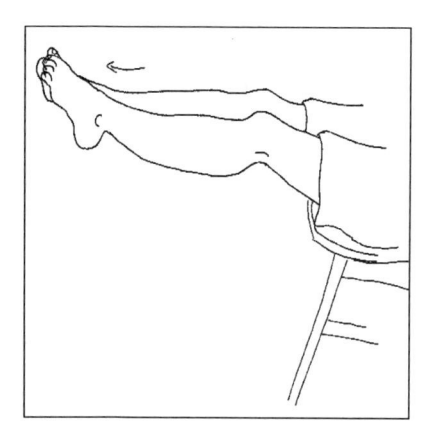 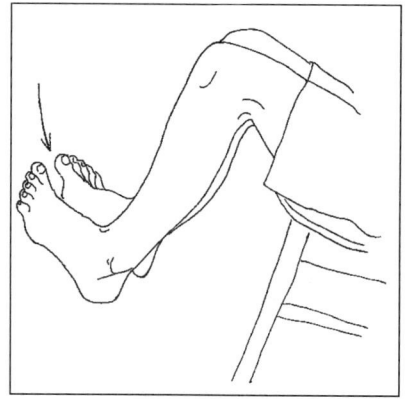

The next set of muscles to concentrate on are the thighs. For this simply extend both your legs out in front of you as straight as you can (if this is uncomfortable do one leg at a time). Remember to leave your calves loose – do not tense them. Hold your legs out.... Feel the tension in the thigh muscles ... hold it. ... and relax. Let the feet fall gently to the floor. Focus on the sensations.

Repeat this exercise once more.

To work the opposite set of muscles raise your toes slightly and dig your heels down into the floor as hard as you can. Hold it, focussing on the tension.... and relax.

Again ... pressing down even harder this time ... Relax.

Concentrate on the feeling of relaxation.

To tense the stomach, hold your breath and push it down into the stomach. Make your stomach hard, as if preparing for someone to hit you there with their fist. Hold it like this and notice the tension .... Relax ..... Breathe normally.

Again ... Making the stomach even harder this time ... Hold it... Relax ... Breathe normally, and focus on the feeling of relaxation spreading over the thighs and all through the stomach area.

Hands and Arms

 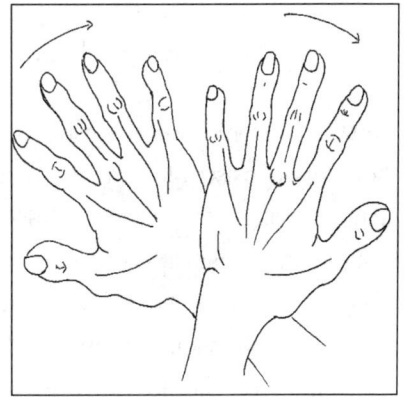

Now you move on to the hands. The first thing to do is to make very tight fists — clench them as hard as you can. Feel the tension over the knuckles and into the lower arms. Hold it. And relax.

Repeat this once more. Make the fists even tighter. ... Hold it ... Relax ....

This exercise is excellent when you have a lot of writing to do.
To work the opposite muscles, spread your fingers as wide as you can.
Widen them out as much as possible ... Hold it ... Relax.
Again .... Spreading the fingers even wider ... Relax.
Concentrate on the warmth or tingling in your hands and forearms.

Shoulders

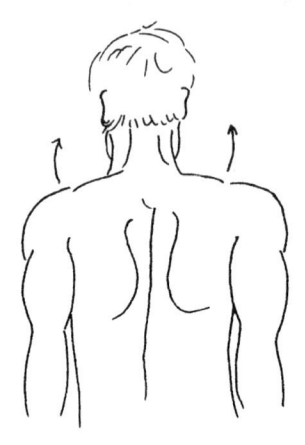

We tend to store a lot of tension in our shoulders. The exercise for the shoulders consists of shrugging your shoulders up towards your ears. Imagine trying to touch your earlobes with the tops of your shoulders. Bring them up high.... Feel the tension in the shoulders..... Hold it.... and relax. Let the shoulders go loose and heavy.

Again. Lift your shoulders up even higher.... Hold it.... Relax.

Concentrate on the heaviness in your shoulders. Let them relax even more, go heavier and heavier.

Face

Lastly, the muscles of the face, starting with the mouth. Smile as widely as you can — very wide – an ear-to-ear grin. Hold it and feel the tension. Now relax. Repeat once more.

The opposite set of muscles are tensed by puckering up your lips as if you were going to give someone a kiss. Pucker as tightly as you can. Hold it ... and relax. Once again.

Now up to the eyes (be sure to remove contact lenses). Keeping your eyes closed, clench them very tightly. Hold it .... and relax. Again, squeezing them even more tightly shut... feel the tension.... now relax.

And finally the muscles of the forehead and scalp. Lift your eyebrows as high as you can, keeping your eyes closed. Hold it like that. Relax. And again – lifting the eyebrows even higher, and relax. Concentrate on the feeling of relaxation that has spread all through the face muscles.

Deepening

Now you have relaxed most of the major muscles in your body. Let's see if you can relax them even more deeply. Go over the muscles in your mind and think about letting them get even more relaxed – your forehead, eyes, cheeks – relaxed .... your neck, shoulders, chest and stomach – more and more relaxed .... your thigh muscles, calves and down into your feet – the pleasant feeling of relaxation. Your whole body feels relaxed, a warm glow passes over you, and you feel good. Spend a few moments enjoying this feeling.

Alerting

Now you will count back slowly from 10 to 1, and when you get to 1 you will open your eyes.. With each number you will feel more alert. 10...9...8 - you are becoming more awake ... 7... 6 ... 5 – start to stretch your arms ...4 ... 3 .... 2... – start to stretch your legs ....1 ... open your eyes.

You are now feeling alert and refreshed.

9. CONTROLLED BREATHING

Voluntary control of breathing as a method of reducing anxiety and promoting a state of relaxation dates back thousands of years. Centuries before Christ this stress-reduction technique was used, and continued to be used in various forms, right up to the present day. The most widely used form today is the procedure for "natural childbirth".

While voluntary breath control is an effective and flexible aid to anxiety reduction, it should be used with caution. One must guard against overbreathing, or hyperventilation. Long pauses after inhaling and exhaling should be avoided. Inhaling and exhaling should be a smooth, steady procedure, without strain or discomfort. The breathing exercises should be used for short periods of time (not longer than 5-10 minutes). Stop if you feel a sensation of light-headedness or tingling.

Breathing Exercises

1. *Inhalation*: The inhalation should begin through the nose if possible. The nose is preferable to the mouth because it can filter and warm the incoming air. As you inhale, the abdomen should begin to move outward, followed by expansion of the chest. The length of the inhalation should be two to three seconds (or to some point less than where the lungs and chest expand without discomfort).
2. Do not pause after inhalation. Inhalation should transfer smoothly into exhalation.
3. *Exhalation*: Here the air is expired (through the mouth or the nose, whichever is more comfortable). The length of this exhalation should be two to three seconds.
4. Pause after exhalation. This pause should last only one second, then inhalation should begin again in a smooth manner.
   This exercise can be repeated for up to 10 minutes, but stop if light-headness occurs.

4. THE EXAM ITSELF

10. EXAM DAY

Good exam technique is vitally important. Up to 15% can be gained by proper exam know-how. When you translate this into actual results it means that you could improve by a whole grade by knowing and using good exam skills. Practiced well over the academic year, these skills will be automatic when the day of the exam arrives. This chapter will consider the most important aspects of dealing with the written paper.

Night Before The Exam

1. Make out a list of all the equipment you will need, including such items as biros (blue, black, green and red), black and coloured pencils, ruler, eraser, mathematical set (if necessary), calculator, etc. Any other necessities or extras should also go on the list (e.g. watch, tissues, drink).
   This will be your checklist for the following morning.
2. Get everything on your list and check that all equipment is working properly.
3. To refresh your memory, spend about one hour skimming over your tables or notes. **Learn nothing new at this stage**.
4. Get to bed early, 10.30 to 11.00 p.m. A hot relaxing bath prior to retiring to bed will give you a feeling of relaxation and help you to sleep. Relaxation exercises (Chapter 7) will also help.
5. For some days before the exams insomnia is a common occurrence. Do not worry about this. (Refer to chapter 13).
6. Make arrangements to ensure that you will get up two hours before the exam the following morning, to avoid rushing.

Morning Of The Exam

When you wake on exam day you are sure to feel a sense of something different. Your body will tell you that the big day has arrived. You are likely to feel one or more of the following: "Butterflies" in your stomach and maybe even a slightly sick feeling, fast breathing, rapid pulse rate, tension in your muscles, a slight headache like a tight band around your head. These feelings are quite normal and understandable. After all, you have planned and worked for this day and every student will have some doubts about how they will manage. But it is not these feelings that are important. What matters is how you react to them, deal with them and manage them.

Your first step on waking on exam day is to acknowledge any feelings of nervous tension and to reassure yourself that it is quite normal to feel this way. This is what you expected, and these feelings can actually help you to give your best performance. You should talk to yourself using your positive self-statements, "This is what I expected ... This is normal.... It's only exam tension and it's harmless... A lot of this is really just excitement.... I can manage the tension .... Even if it goes very high it will come down again ...".

Having reassured yourself about what is happening, your next step is to do some deep relaxation. Spend 10 minutes on deep muscular relaxation (Chapter 7). After this it may help to have a quick, cool shower to freshen up for the day ahead. You are now ready for a light breakfast (e.g. cereal, tea with sugar and toast). Do not have large meals such as grills, etc. Avoid discussing the exam with your family, apart from the necessary practicalities such as travel arrangements.

Before leaving home go through your checklist and make sure that you have everything on it to bring with you.

If you find your anxiety level rising to an uncomfortable level on the way to the exam centre, take out your coping cards (Chapter 6) and read through them slowly. Do your controlled breathing (Chapter 7). Think of the treat you have planned for when the exam is over.

If you are doing the second level State exams most people find it easier to wear their school uniform. It gives them a feeling of familiarity. They have done this several times already and have undertaken exams in this very school, wearing this very uniform. It puts them in the mood for work.

When you arrive you will see some people buried in books; others eagerly asking friends for some last minute information; others will be complaining about how they feel, and a few will be laughing and joking as though they have no anxiety whatsoever. Avoid any groups who are either involved in last minute revision or discussing their nerves. Stay by yourself preferably, and keep reassuring yourself that you have prepared well.

The Paper

Until you are involved in answering the exam questions, when nervous tension will fade away, you must do your best to confront and control any negative thoughts. Examples of the types of negative anxiety-producing thoughts might be anticipating panic or "going blank", worrying about your performance compared to others, agonizing over the consequences of doing badly, or being preoccupied with bodily sensations related to stress. Challenge these thoughts and provide yourself with the rational answers that you have practiced beforehand. Also, use the early feelings of tension as your cue to use your relaxation techniques. These will keep tension levels under control.

When you get the paper:

1. Check the instructions precisely, in case there is a change in exam format from the previous year.
2. Read each question carefully. Highlight and underline the important words.
3. Check again how many questions must be answered in each section, and read each question again, putting a tick mark beside all those you might attempt. Now choose those you will answer, marking them clearly.
4. Allot time for each answer. This is vitally important, and should have been worked out before you sit the exam. How much time you allow for each question will depend mainly on the marks given for each question. Allow five minutes at the start for reading the paper, and ten minutes at the end for checking over answers. Don't go over the allotted time. Three good answers amount to more marks than two very good answers.

5. Start with the question you are most comfortable with. This will get you into the flow of the paper and give you confidence. It also gives the examiner a good initial impression.

6. Plan out each answer clearly before you begin. Put down the main points to be included, making an outline of the answer. Put this in an obvious position and label it clearly, so that if you run out of time the examiner can see how you were progressing.

7. Label your answer and every page to avoid confusion.

8. Write clearly, with big script if possible. The examiner will appreciate an easily read answer.

9. Use your coloured biros to highlight your answer, e.g. blue to write with, green for your subheadings, red for the main headings and black for underlining words of importance in the answer itself.

10. Leaving a line between each paragraph of an essay-type answer can help to make things clearer.

11. Leave a few lines between answers and start each section on a new page or answerbook.

12. If you run out of time on a question, leave a big space and go right on to the next one. You may have time to get back to it later, and if not, two half-finished questions will get you more marks than one completed answer.

13. Don't waffle. Examiners don't want one answer in ten different ways. Keep to the point and be as concise as possible in factual answers.

14. Diagrams must always have a heading. Likewise, graph axes must be labelled, or marks can be lost.

15. Diagrams should be large, and drawn in pencil. Use two or three colours, but do not use more. It isn't a colouring competition!

16. If noises distract you, use earplugs. Remember you only have one chance at the exam and blaming someone for making noise won't get you better marks.

17. To avoid dehydration, bring a drink with you into the exam hall, e.g. orange juice.

18. Never leave the exam hall until the time is up. You never know what might spring to mind in the final minutes.

As you work through the paper keep it clean (no doodles, finger marks, blotches of ink or careless erasing), and keep your writing neat and legible. The examiner will appreciate an easily read paper and may be more sympathetic in a case where your answer could do with a kind eye.

When you have answered all questions, see how much time is left on the clock. If there are some unfinished answers, you now divide the rest of the time (except for 10 minutes for checking at the end), among these unfinished answers. Try to complete each one, if not in detail then in outline form. Use headings and abbreviated sentences if time is running out.

Don't stop working on your paper until the time is fully up. Each moment is precious. You won't get any extra marks for being finished early, but you may lose some by failing to check over your work, more than once if you have time. Read the exam paper again. Have you answered all questions? Have you answered one too many? If so then cross out the answer you are least happy with. Read over your answers carefully. Neatly add in any extra important points and make any changes or corrections.

If you discover that you have misread a question or left one out, you must remember that this often happens to people doing exams and most of them get through anyway. Use positive self-statements to keep yourself in command of the situation, such as "I can cope with this .....This is just another challenge....I will use my energy to make out some answer...." etc. Sketch an outline of an answer first, and then fill in main headings and abbreviated sentences. If it is a mathematical problem, the same applies – sketch out the steps firstly, and then do calculations if you have time.

As you finally put down your pen and hand in your paper take time to say to yourself "Well done ... I met the challenge ... I gave it my best shot".

When The Exam Is Over ...

If the exam didn't go according to plan, confront and control any negative anxiety-producing thoughts. Maybe you forgot to allot time to each question. Perhaps you spent too much time on the essay. Maybe you allowed yourself to daydream during the last 10 minutes instead of rechecking the paper. Instead of feeling angry with yourself or fearing the worst, you can learn from this mistake and make the necessary changes at the next paper.

Avoid lengthy post-mortems. You possibly have another exam in the afternoon or the next day. If you get involved with discussions on the paper just completed you will almost certainly discover that you left something out or that you made some mistake, and this is likely to become the focus of your attention.

No matter how well or badly you feel you have done, leave the exam centre and treat yourself for having got through according to plan.

You must now begin preparing for the next exam. It may be on a different subject altogether. You will have a chance to start again. Each paper is a fresh start and, most importantly, a new examiner. Let the completed paper drift from your mind. Forget the material you knew that didn't come up or was forgotten. Let your disappointment ebb away. Every student, no matter how brilliant, will feel that they could have done better if only they had...... That is the exam system.

When you return home in the evenings, discuss the paper in more detail with a sympathetic adult. This can be a parent, brother, sister, or any relative. While they may not be totally familiar with the subject on hand they can listen, and give a balanced view of your performance.

If your exams are second level National examinations you should keep in touch with the national response to each paper in the daily newspapers, radio, etc. These columns give advice on the points system generally, and also give a daily summary of the country-wide response to each subject as the exams proceed. If you feel a particular question was unfair, contact these columnists. They will investigate the problem and contact the Department of Education if deemed necessary. Do not wait for others to do this – make it your own responsibility. Keeping in touch with the national response gives a broader, more objective perspective. Your teacher may have focussed on a particular section of a subject. You need to get a feeling of the overall view.

Each exam evening

- Put away your notes and books on the exam undertaken. Don't be tempted to check up on anything
- Do a short revision of the next day's subject's
- Focus on main headings only
- Learn nothing new
- Avoid discussions with classmates, in person or on the phone
- If you feel negative about the paper that you have just completed, a shower and relaxation exercises will help to relieve your tension
- Retire early

11. ESSAYS, ORALS, AURALS AND MCQs

ESSAYS

The essay is a very important question on any paper. Therefore, it is essential to do it well.

This is the time when you are working on your own initiative. Therefore, you need to be able to produce a variety of ideas. A good method of producing concepts is called "Brainstorming" (see Chapter 3). On seeing a title, write down, in any order, as many ideas as you can think of that are associated with it. Spend about ten minutes doing this. Then read down through your ideas. Dismiss any that you feel are too weak or not entirely relevant. Remember, it is far easier to discard ideas than to come up with new ones, so the greater number of points that you produce during the brainstorming stage the better.

Once you have the main ideas you intend to use for your essay, spend ten minutes organising them. Allow each main heading to be used for a paragraph. Take each heading and write down in a little more detail the point(s) you intend to make under this heading. Next decide in what order you will write the paragraphs. You must try to have a connection between one paragraph and the next. This is important, so that the examiner can see a logical train of thought in your essay.

Try to have a minimum of six, and a maximum of nine paragraphs in the essay (not including the introduction or conclusion).

The introduction is perhaps the most important part of the essay. Here you win the examiner's interest, approval or criticism. It is up to you to come up with some interesting anecdote, startling statistic, eye-catching statement, thought-provoking question, etc., to make the examiner realise that your essay is not simply one of the rest. This is essential. It is difficult to gain the examiner's interest after a poor opening, or to lose it after an interesting one.

The conclusion of the essay is also vitally important. You are making your final impression before you receive your mark for the essay. Even if you have little else to add, summarise the main ideas of your essay. End with a quotation or question – literally any method you can think of, to leave the examiner with a memorable impression of your essay. Remember marks are also awarded for spelling and structure, as well as for imagination and style. During the year, read as much as possible outside the curriculum. This will help you to develop your own inidividual style.

Although the essay is produced by you, rather than learned from books, it is vital to practice. Two or three times a week practice the brainstorming method yourself, coming up with as many ideas as possible, then discarding irrelevant ones, and organising paragraphs. Once every two weeks it is necessary to write out a full essay, under exam conditions. If your teacher/lecturer doesnt' tell you to do this, pick out a title for yourself from previous exam papers. This work will be invaluable when the day of the examination arrives.

Keep your writing large and clear. Many students and teachers find it a help to skip a line after each paragraph to ensure that the page is not too cluttered. Vary your sentences between long and short for variety. If your sentence is too long the reader may lose its meaning. Try to limit sentence length to about three lines of an A4 page.

Make sure that you keep the title of the essay in mind throughout. Short essay-type answers are also required for other exam questions. You should be familiar with the commonly used terms in such questions and abide by them in your answer. The following list includes some of these terms.

Compare	Describe the similarities and differences.
Contrast	Point out the differences.
Define	State clearly and concisely the facts involved.
Describe	Trace out and give a general account of.
Discuss	Debate, giving arguments for and against.
Explain	Account for and interpret.
Evaluate	Judge the value or importance of.
Illustrate	Demonstrate clearly (use diagrams where suitable).
Trace	Give an account of, from start to finish.
Summarise/Outline	Give a precise, brief account of the main points, or briefly state the general plan.

ORALS

Find out exactly the percentage of the total exam alotted to the oral in question (it can vary from 10% in some subjects to 25% in others). For orals it is absolutely useless to merely cram the week beforehand. Practice is the way to win. From the beginning of the school year students should set aside a particular amount of time each week for the orals, gradually increasing it as the orals themselves approach.

Orals are believed to be the easiest area in examinations to gain marks. Try to speak Irish/German/French/Italian/Spanish to friends. Get your classmates to co-operate and set aside one lunchtime each week solely for this purpose. Any interested students can get together and speak in the chosen language. Some students may feel ambivalent about doing this at first, but once you get started you will find yourself joining in quite readily. Those who are not participating are missing out. Similarly, at home, encourage your family to try to speak Irish, French, etc. Practice is essential in order to develop fluency.

Prior to the orals you should have notes prepared on obvious topics. The usual questions are based on

- Family structure (occupation of parents, brothers and sisters, etc.)
- Personal ambitions, interests and pastimes
- Where you live, advantages and disadvantages of the area, industries, etc.
- Previous holidays taken, whether you were in the Gaeltacht, whether you went abroad. You may be asked to compare the place where you last spent a holiday with your home town
- General topics such as unemployment, emigration, smoking, drinking, pollution, nuclear energy, etc.
- Current affairs. Keep up-to-date by reading magazines and newspapers (especially editorials). Magazines such as "Anois" and "Authentik" deal with current matters on a basic level

Notes on topics are extremely helpful, but do not learn off paragraphs. Remember that an oral exam is conducted by very experienced teachers who can easily spot a word-for-word learned piece. If an examiner thinks that you have memorised sentences, he/she will simply change the topic. You may then have lost the opportunity to speak on a prepared topic, thereby losing precious marks.

For approximately six weeks leading up to the orals, take note of what is happening in the world at large. Have key words translated into the language required. Always keep in mind that an oral exam is a conversation not an interview.

When the actual oral arrives, try to be as relaxed as possible (see Chapter 7). Remember that you are just going to chat with a stranger for a short while. Oral examiners are going to award high marks to any student who just converses naturally. It shows great command of the language.

Dress neatly. Smile appropriately when you enter the interview room. Make eye contact with your examiner and try to avoid looking elsewhere while answering. If you find direct eye contact difficult because of nervousness, look at your examiner at eyebrow level – he/she will not know the difference. Take time with your answers. If you are unsure of the meaning of the question or a particular word ask the examiner to repeat the question, or explain the word. The examiner will be helpful. Let the conversation develop naturally. Don't try to introduce prepared topics which are inappropriate at that time. Many students try to lead the examiner to a certain topic by wearing such things as CND badges, etc. Try it if you wish, but don't depend on it. Be sensible about your hobbies. Discuss pastimes that you are familiar with.

At the end of the oral the examiner will indicate that it is drawing to a close. Be courteous. Thank your examiner.

AURALS

Throughout the year aurals should be practised at least once a week. You should have sample tapes and should practise listening and answering the questions. Spend at least half an hour on this each week, in addition to class aurals. Know the exact percentage of marks that the aural exam will be worth.

In class and in the examination hall sit as close to the tape as possible. If you have a hearing disability, the Department of Education will make special arrangements to provide you with special facilities. The school/college authorities will know the procedure and must be informed at least three months before the examination itself.

At the exam, the paper is handed out approximately five minutes before the tape is played. Use this time to read the instructions for each section. The tape is then played to the whole room. The instructions vary from section to section and you will be informed of this on the tape or on the written paper. Make sure you have noted how often the conversation will be played in each section. Sit and listen during the first play. Do not attempt to answer the questions unless the answer is very obvious. The section will be played a second time and often will be split up into parts.

Answer the questions on the second playing.

Use the third playing (if any) to check your answers carefully.

MCQs

With the gradual modernisation of our exam system, Multiple Choice Questions (MCQs) have become a popular method of examination in both second and third level education. This is because they are easy to correct, are objectively scored, and require fairly detailed knowledge of the subject.

The MCQ can be presented in a variety of ways. The usual format is to have one question with two or more answers. The student must choose the most suitable response. Check the instructions carefully as they can vary greatly from paper to paper.

The MCQs can be marked positively or negatively. The latter is used especially in third level exams.

Positively Marked MCQs

Here you are rewarded for a correct answer but not penalised for an incorrect one. Therefore, you should attempt all of the questions as you have nothing to lose.

Negatively Marked MCQs

Here you are rewarded for correct answers but are penalised for incorrect ones. The penalty varies, for example:

	Bonus	Penalty
	(for correct choice)	(for incorrect choice)
	+1	− 1
or	+1	− ·5

Find out the exact penalty before the exam. If this is impossible, acquire the information before touching your answer sheet.

A suggested method for answering MCQs is as follows:

1. Go through the paper the first time, answering the questions you are certain of. Put a mark beside the questions which you are unsure of, but have studied.

2. On the second run through, answer the questions which you have marked, if you can. The chances are that you will make the correct choice.

3. If your exam is positively marked it is safe to attempt the rest of the questions, as you continue to increase your chances of a correct answer. However, if your exam is negatively marked, do not attempt what you don't know, even if this means leaving 30-35% of your questions unanswered. Guessing could easily cause you to fail.

In doing MCQs you should not be tempted to change your original answers. Psychologically, the more you see something, the more familiar it will appear to you. You may feel that you have seen a statement before by the third or fourth time you have read the questions. Follow your original hunches.

Finally, the best way to prepare for MCQs is to practise.
MCQ books are available with in most educational bookshops.
Attempt them under exam conditions and be strict with yourself.

5. HEALTH

12. HEALTHY HABITS

Students undertaking state exams are usually in their mid to late adolescence (15 - 22 years). During these formative years major changes take place both biologically and psychologically. To mature to adulthood, and survive the academic pressures set up by schools, colleges, universities and peers is no mean feat. The students themselves try to live up to their parents' expectations on the one hand, while establishing their own identity on the other. Most students outgrow these vulnerable years without trauma. Yet, while parents and schools pay great attention to academic achievement, scant attention is paid to a fundamental aspect of the student's whole existence, i.e. his/her health.

DIET

The word diet does not simply mean a method of losing weight. In the 1990s young people, especially girls, have become obsessed with their figures, comparing themselves to the models they see and read about in magazines. "Fad diets" have recently become such a craze that two per cent of today's teenagers suffer from recognised eating disorders such as Anorexia Nervosa and Bulimia Nervosa. These conditions will be discussed in the next chapter. The basic problem with the Fad Diets one reads about in magazines, is that they don't supply the body and brain with sufficient energy or raw materials to function at its best.

For example, without sufficient minerals such as Iron, Vit. B12, Vit. C etc., anaemia develops, causing tiredness. When preparing for exams, following a fad diet is like stabbing yourself in the back. Unless your diet is a medically monitored one, because of a major weight problem, avoid dieting altogether. In fact, most students find that they lose weight gradually over the teen years. Loss of "puppy fat" is a favourite way of describing this natural process as the body grows and develops. During the academic year and the actual exam period itself, great stress and energy is generated, causing a further weight loss. An adequate and nutritious diet must be maintained for you to perform well and excel in your studies.

The following Table gives the recommended weight ranges for males and females, based on height.

Recommended Weights for Males and Females		
Height Ft. Ins	Male Weight Lbs	Female Weight Lbs
5 - 1	108 - 120	100 - 111
5 - 2	113 - 126	103 - 114
5 - 3	118 - 131	108 - 121
5 - 4	123 - 136	113 - 126
5 - 5	128- 141	115 - 129
5 - 6	133 - 146	120 - 133
5 - 7	136 - 151	123 - 137
5 - 8	140 - 156	128 - 142
5 - 9	146 - 162	133 - 147
5 -10	151 - 167	138 - 152
5 -11	158 - 174	147- 161
6 - 0	166 - 182	
6 - 1	171 - 185	
6 - 2	173 - 191	
6 - 3	175 - 198	
6 - 4	181 - 201	
6 - 5	188- 209	

Your dietary intake must be sufficient to maintain the metabolic requirements of your body. Protein, carbohydrates, fats, vitamins, minerals and fibre are all distributed in different proportions in various foods. The right dietary balance must be adhered to, to ensure healthy living.

Energy is stored in food and is released in the form of Calories.

	Calories
Protein (1 gram)	4
Carbohydrate (1 gram)	4
Fat (1 gram)	9

Your body should receive approx. 15% of its energy from Protein, 35% from Fat and 50% from Carbohydrate. One must always remember that dietary preferences may vary from country to country. Daily energy

Calorie Content in Different Foods	
FOOD	**CALORIES** per 100 Grams
Fruit	
Apples	65
Oranges	50
Strawberries	40
Vegetables	
Potatoes	83
Peas	100
Spinach	25
Carrots	48
Meat	
Beef	270
Lamb	240
Pork	350
Chicken	115
Fish	
Haddock	80
Cheese	
Cheddar	400
Chocolate	
Plain milk	550
Bread	
White (fresh)	270
Milk	
Whole Milk	70

requirements vary from person to person, depending on size, age, sex, weight. The Basal Metabolic Rate (B.M.R.) is the amount of energy you need to stay alive, while lying in bed all day. The standard example is of a 70 kg. man, whose requirements would be approximately 1650 calories per day.

Any other activity, such as working, walking, exercising, dressing, standing, etc., means that more calories will be expended and your diet should be adjusted upwards accordingly, e.g. eating and digestion – 220 calories per day.

In this country, males aged between 15-20 years require a minimum of 3000 calories per day. Equivalent females require a minimum of 2200 calories per day. These values are those recommended for adolescents who are moderately active, e.g. students.

A BALANCED DIET SHOULD CONTAIN THE FOLLOWING

1. Protein

Approximately 12-15% of your total energy should come from protein. This is especially important in teenagers for growth, repair and renewal of tissue. Sources include meat, fish, eggs, nuts, etc.

2. Carbohydrate

This is the important energy source of your diet and should make up 40 - 50 per cent of your total dietary intake. White bread contains 2.5g carbohydrate per 100 grams. Remember that fruit contains carbohydrate also.

3. Fats

Many teenagers try to cut down on fats, but, in fact, fats should constitute a **minimum of 20 per cent and a maximum of 30 per cent of your diet**. With regard to the current topic of saturated fats versus polyunsaturates, it is safe to say that a certain amount of both is ideal.

4. *Vitamins and Minerals*

The following table lists the most important vitamins and minerals which you need daily in your diet. Students often neglect to take an adequate supply:

Vitamins	Sources	Symptoms of Vitamin/ Mineral Deficiency
A	Carrots, Fish Liver Oils	Night blindness
B1 (Thiamine)	Yeast, Meat, Wheatgerm	Colds Gastro-intestinal disorders
B2 (Riboflavin)	Liver, Yeast	Lack of energy Mental Depression Forgetfulness
B6 (Niacin)	Meat, Yeast extract (e.g. Marmite)	Mental Problems Skin conditions
C (Ascorbic Acid)	Fruits	Skin conditions Dental Decay
D	Cheese, Eggs, Milk	Dental decay
Ca (Calcium)	Milk	Dental and gum decay
Fe (Iron)	Meat	Anaemia, low energy, susceptibility to infection

If you feel that your own diet falls short, especially with regard to the nutrients in this Table, multivitamin and mineral supplements would be a good investment. Current hype regarding vitamins improving one's intelligence has proven to be false.

In recent surveys it has been shown that one multivitamin and mineral supplement taken daily, may increase your energy and efficiency for study purposes.

5. Fibre   Fibre is important in ensuring smooth functioning of the digestive system.

About 25-50g daily is an adequate amount, and it is especially high in cereals such as bran, potatoes, rice, etc.

6. Liquids   In order to keep your head clear, to avoid headaches and to concentrate properly, a student should drink approximately three litres of fluid daily. Coffee, much loved by students, deserves a special mention as a liquid source. It has unpleasant side effects that the student may overlook. (See Chapter 13).

HOW TO CHOOSE AN ADEQUATE DIET

You might think from the above that choosing foods that will ensure an adequate nutritious diet is a rather complex process. Fortunately, this is not so. Choosing a balanced, healthy diet is very simple. Just follow the guidelines in the following Table:

Suggested Meal Plan
1. Have three meals per day.
2. Plenty of vegetables, including potatoes, (one or two servings).
3. Fruit, as much as you desire (at least two servings).
4. No calorie counting.
5. Full three course dinner.
6. One vitamin supplement, if necessary.
7. Avoid large quantities of caffeine.
8. Avoid binge eating.
9. Two glasses of milk. Two or three litres of water daily.

The term "Serving" has the ordinary, everyday meaning, e.g.

bread = 2-3 slices
meat = 3 oz etc.

13. UNHEALTHY HABITS

EATING DISORDERS

Now that diet has been discussed, including the importance of establishing normal and regular eating patterns, eating disorders should not be overlooked.

The main eating disorders suffered by teenagers are:
1. *Anorexia Nervosa*
2. *Bulimia Nervosa*

One cannot stress too forcibly the fact that anorexia nervosa and bulimia nervosa are recognised disorders. The student with a calorific intake which balances the calorific output does not suffer from these potentially fatal illnesses. The student with normal eating patterns do not have to worry about what they eat, nor about these two diseases. Yet it is sad to say that approximately 2 per cent of adolescents in this country suffer from one of these eating disorders.

A preoccupation with thinness goes back decades, but really reached peak proportions only in the 1980s. The media must bear much of the responsibility for this unfortunate situation. Advertisers recognised the trend towards preoccupation with thinness and, in order to sell their magazines and newspapers, included at least one article per issue on diet/reducing weight in most journals. There has been a 50 per cent increase in articles on diet in the U.K. over the past 10 years. In a recent survey in the U.K. 45 per cent of schoolgirls considered themselves overweight, while 35 per cent were actively dieting. There is no reason to believe that girls in Ireland are any different.

FACTS ABOUT ANOREXIA NERVOSA

- A disease mainly of adolescence. Age of onset can occur from 10 to 30 years, but is most frequent at about the age of 15 to 18 years
- It is 20 times more common in girls
- There is an all-consuming preoccupation with diet
- A diet plan is undertaken and rigidly adhered to
- Fear of weight gain
- Calorie counting – daily intake, etc.
- Becoming anorexic (decreasing one's appetite)
- Skipping meals – frequent excuses for this

In three to six months:

- They lose their appetite
- They avoid family meals, may be binge-eating and hide food during meals if others are showing concern for them
- Deny weight loss, even when emaciated
- They are preoccupied with body image, especially of thighs, feel that their stomach is protruding and that their breasts are excessive
- They deny that it is a problem – frequent arguments with parents
- They increase exercise, usually exercising alone
- They commonly engage in self-induced vomiting
- Their periods stop
- DEATH IN 10 PER CENT OF CASES

There are, of course, the detrimental effects on study:

- Time is spent on preoccupation with food, dieting and exercise
- Insomnia
- Fainting episodes
- Headaches
- Listlessness, fatigue and tiring easily

Students with anorexia nervosa will ridicule the suggestion that they actually have an eating disorder. They will deny their obvious weight reduction. In order to keep their obsession with reducing food intake secret, they will blame the family, stress at school, study, etc., when challenged. It is a great struggle for most parents to come to terms with this problem. Unfortunately, by the time they accept that serious problems have arisen, the disease is usually firmly established.

Education is by far the best approach to anorexia nervosa. A child is never too young to start learning about healthy eating habits. Biology and Home Economics courses have helped to broaden this understanding in recent years.

BULIMIA NERVOSA

Anorexia nervosa and Bulimia nervosa can co-exist. Bulimia nervosa is charactised by uncontrolled binge eating. The individual may have a rapid ingestion of massive quantities of food which are consumed voraciously. Nausea and abdominal pain will usually bring about the end of the actual binge. Self-induced vomiting is typically carried out following the binge. The person will feel guilty and full of self-disgust. Like anorexia nervosa it is more common in females. Studies in the U.S.A. have shown that bulimia nervosa can occur in as many as 35 per cent of college girls.

Like anorexia nervosa, bulimia nervosa students are usually high achievers. Their families may suffer from conflict and depression more frequently than the families of anorexia nervosa sufferers.

SYMPTOMS OF BULIMIA NERVOSA

- Preoccupation with weight and body image
- Episodes of binge eating
- Massive quantities of food are eaten
- Self-induced vomiting
- Abdominal bloating and pain
- Food is usually of carbohydrate type, such as chocolate and cake
- Body image disturbance
- Denial of possible depression

Bulimia nervosa may go on for years. The student may function well between relapses. It is rarely fatal.

The following graph gives the student a rough guide to acceptable weight levels.

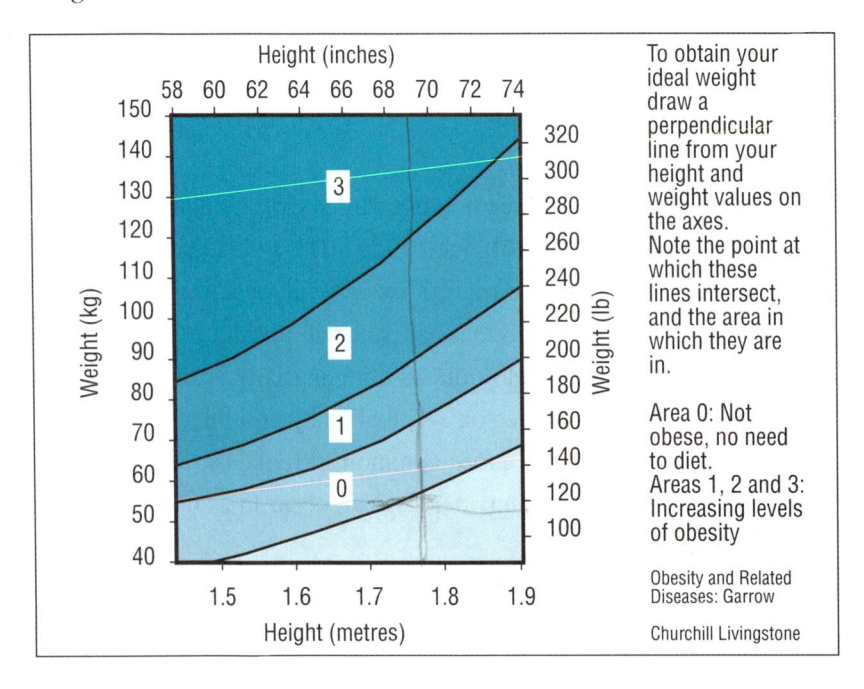

To obtain your ideal weight draw a perpendicular line from your height and weight values on the axes. Note the point at which these lines intersect, and the area in which they are in.

Area 0: Not obese, no need to diet.
Areas 1, 2 and 3: Increasing levels of obesity

Obesity and Related Diseases: Garrow

Churchill Livingstone

CAFFEINE

Most students drink large quantities of caffeine. This may be in the form of coffee, tea, coke, 7UP, Pepsi, chocolate, etc. A cup of coffee contains 150 mg. of caffeine. Small quantities will cause students to be more alert and give a sense of well- being.

Large quantities may cause insomnia, headaches, nausea, or vomiting. Some people will become tense and anxious if too much caffeine is taken over a long period of time.

Common sources of caffeine:

Coffee	150 mg. of caffeine per unit (1 cup)
Tea	100 mg. of caffeine per unit (1 cup)
Chocolate Bar	50 mg. of caffeine per unit (2 oz. bar)
7UP, Pepsi, etc.	50 mg. of caffeine per unit (1 glass)

You should be aware that those who take high levels of caffeine develop a dependency, just like nicotine users. Cessation of either brings about unpleasant symptoms, causing havoc with studies. Prior to exams, students increase their caffeine intake and thereby become more restless, nervous and agitated. They sleep poorly and develop gastro-intestinal disturbances. They are, therefore, at a distinct disadvantage when facing the exam paper. If you like the taste of coffee you can switch to a decaffeinated variety.

Avoid caffeine tablets. They cause agitation, anxiety and confusion. You will be unable to concentrate, and your studies will suffer accordingly.

INSOMINA

Sleep disturbance is common amongst young people, occurring in five to ten per cent of the student population. Most people feel eight hours sleep is sufficient for the body to relax and restore the energy lost during an active day. Individuals may differ in their sleep requirements, yet seven to ten hours is adequate in the vast majority of cases. The object of sleep is to wake in the morning feeling renewed and refreshed to face a working day.

Lack of sleep will lead to a feeling of tiredness which will affect concentration and cause recent memory deterioration. The student may develop headaches, leading to irritability and difficulty in performing well at their studies.

FACTORS CAUSING DIFFICULTY IN FALLING ASLEEP

Anxiety	This may be due to an upcoming anxiety-provoking situation (e.g. exams, job interview). It may also occur once the stressful situation has passed. The person becomes restless on retiring to bed and has great difficulty in falling asleep. Sometimes the person has difficulty remaining asleep.
Tension	Going directly from study to bed may not only make it difficult to "switch off" mentally, but muscles are also likely to be tense.
Uncomfortable conditions	Cold, damp, unfamiliar surroundings, etc.
Pain	E.g. headaches, abdominal pain, arthritis, pre-menstrual tension.
Diets	Insufficient dietary intake to maintain healthy living results in insomnia. Starvation diets are strongly associated with insomnia.
Drugs	Alcohol, particularly when excessive amounts are taken. Alcohol withdrawal symptoms. Marijuana,Opiates, Caffeine, etc.
Depression	This type of sleeping difficulty is usually associated with early morning wakening. There may be a

	normal sleep onset but the person wakes at 3 or 4 a.m.
Sleep Apnoea	This is associated with tonsils and adenoids. There is an obstructed airway for 10 to 20 seconds, causing difficulty in breathing. This disturbs the person's sleep several times throughout the night..
Change in night sleep/wake routine	Students studying excessively late into the night. jet lag, night shift job, etc., all disturb normal sleep patterns.
Physical conditions	Colds, coughs, asthma, headaches, etc.

MANAGEMENT

1. Retire to bed and rise at the same time each day.
2. Avoid stimulants, e.g. coffee, tea, nicotine in the later evening hours.
3. Alcohol may induce sleep but you may wake during the night about four to five hours later.
4. Daytime naps should be avoided.
5. Regular exercise should be undertaken before late evening.
6. Stimulating events on television and videos are best avoided before bedtime.
7. A short period of relaxed reading in bed, listening to the radio, etc., will promote sleep.
8. Consume your meals at regular times. Large meals prior to retiring are best avoided.
9. Relieve tension by carrying out relaxation exercises (see Chapter 7).
10. Concentrate on pleasant events.
11. If you are lying awake 30 minutes after retiring to bed,   simply get up and do something else. Some people change to another room, relax, read a book, listen to music, etc. Return to bed only when you feel the need.

Sleeping tablets are rarely used nowadays for sleep induction, but in certain cases non-addictive medication is available from your G.P. If the insomnia is prolonged and endangering your health you should seek advice.

SUGGESTIONS

- Remember that food is necessary for vital body functions and energy for work
- Know the ideal weight for your age, sex and height
- Realise that weight fluctuates, and that it varies within each month, especially the week before menstruation
- Physical exercise must be undertaken to perform well at study. Daily exercise if possible, never to excess
- Cigarettes should be avoided. Alcohol and caffeine are also drugs of dependence and should be used carefully.
- Avoid peer pressure regarding diet
- Never binge eat
- Develop a regular sleeping pattern

14. PHYSICAL EXERCISE

Regular exercise is not only necessary for positive and healthy physical living, it also creates a feeling of well-being. Students who have enjoyed exercise during their adolescent years are more in control of their lives. No difficulty is encountered by the very young – when sufficient exercise is generated, both at home and at school, to ensure a healthy body. However, lack of physical exercise can become a problem on entering second level education.

Male schools tend to be more involved in physical exercises than girls or mixed schools. An interest in Gaelic games, rugby, or tennis at an early age tends to carry on into adult life. Of course, a large number of students participate in games with great reluctance. At the age of 12 or 13 years schools usually stand firm and insist on physical exercise for all its students. This should be actively encouraged by parents. It is suggested by those in authority that if the young students are unhappy with game participation then they can give it up after the initial two years. The idea is that when this period expires the student will have developed an enjoyment of the game and the freedom involved. Friends are participating and the urge to win will take over. A student will rarely abandon his football, rugby, etc., once he has developed an interest in it.

Girls schools tend to choose hockey, swimming and basketball. They are more reluctant than boys to participate and may only do so when firm direction is given. Of late, tennis tends to have become more popular, perhaps because of the increased media coverage. All schools should include a variety of organised physical exercises in their school agenda.

The Department of Education ought to lead the way in this serious aspect of student health. Everyone knows the benefits of sport and exercise, but more funding will be needed to supply a good choice of sport to suit each student's individual needs. When one considers the vast amount of money spent by the Department of Health on treating diseases resulting from lack of physical exercise, better value may be obtained if the money was directed toward educating the youth in health and fitness matters.

There is a common misconception that good grades are all that matters in schools. Students go from class, to grinds, to homework, day after day. This life-style alone would cause "burnout" in any student. Obviously, grades are the number one priority, but, since time immemorial, exercise has been shown to be beneficial and necessary for health – both mental and physical.

"Mens Sana in Corpore Sano" – a healthy mind in a healthy body.

Parents should actively encourage their children to take up sport. This doesn't only apply to the school year, but also during the holidays. The "I'm bored" syndrome could be alleviated if the student had a variety of sports in which to participate. Parents' interest and pride in their achievements is a key factor in the early stages, and they should also promote physical activities at a local level.

BENEFITS OF SPORT

- Physical fitness is positively associated with good mental health. It improves one's mood.
- It improves one's self-image.
- Physical exercise helps to rest the mind from thousands of facts and figures, and so it is easier to go back to the books feeling renewed.
- Exercise is associated with a reduction of stress and anxiety.
- It lifts the spirit and provides a feeling of freedom.
- It improves one's posture.
- It improves general health – promotes cardiovascular fitness.
- In game interaction, the setting of goals and working toward them, gives a real sense of meaning and purpose.
- Participating in sport gives an opportunity for social interaction and making new friends. There is also the benefit of sharing and team spirit which is so important in socialisation.

The benefits of various popular physical activities are outlined in the following table.

Popular Physical Activities			
	Calories expended per 30/min.	Aerobic fitness	Flexibility
Walking	100 Cals	**	*
Walking (brisk)	200 Cals	***	*
Swimming	250 Cals	***	***
Jogging	300 Cals	***	*
Rugby/soccer	250 Cals	**	**
Basketball	200 Cals	**	**
Table Tennis	150 Cals	**	**
Cycling	225 Cals	***	**
Squash	250 Cals	**	**
Disco dancing	350 Cals	***	***

*	Mild benefit
**	Moderate benefit
***	Excellent benefit

AEROBIC EXERCISE

There are basically two common forms of exercise – aerobic exercise and body-building and toning exercise. Aerobic exercise is aimed at optimising the efficiency of your heart and lung actions, while body-building exercises are aimed at building up muscle mass and physical strength. Of the two forms of exercise, aerobic exercise is vastly more important for improving and maintaining general health and fitness.

The body, just like any other machine, uses fuel (food) in order to power its activities. The fuel must be burned in order to provide the necessary energy and the burning is effected by combining the food with oxygen, which is breathed in, through the lungs, from the air. Our body is composed of billions of cells and each cell requires both fuel and oxygen. These vital substances are carried to each cell in the blood which is channelled through the intricate circuitry of the circulation (veins and arteries). The pump which moves the blood through the veins and arteries is the heart. As well as carrying vital supplies of food and oxygen to the cells, the blood also picks up waste products from the cells which are carried to the lungs and the kidney for excretion.

It is, therefore, of the greatest importance to have a well-developed heart and lung and circulation system. Aerobic exercise ensures that this overall system is maintained in good condition, i.e. a heart that beats slowly and powerfully, lungs that expand deeply and easily when breathing, and a circulatory system that is well developed. One is physically fit when these systems are working at their best. The commonest forms of aerobic exercise are walking, jogging, running on the spot, swimming and cycling. Walking, jogging and running on the spot will be considered in some detail.

Walking As An Exercise

Walking is the simplest and most natural form of exercise. Even the most unfit student should have no difficulty in undertaking a walking regime. You can simply provide 50 minutes of brisk walking, 4/5 times a week (three miles per walk) within your timetable to be physically fit. You may have to gradually work up to this level of walking.

One doesn't have to make arrangements or travel to get involved. No club membership is required. With just a simple pair of walking shoes you can set off and enjoy the sense of freedom that walking gives you. It is also very relaxing to get outside in the fresh air. One can feel the tension ebb away. Concentration is improved on return and energy is restored to tackle those books, yet again.

Jogging

A more strenuous form of exercise which doesn't involve equipment or club fee, is jogging. In order to be physically fit, one should jog five times a week, each jog of three miles duration, and to be completed in 20/25 minutes. Of course, if you are not already fit, you will have to gradually work up to this level over a period of several weeks.

Both walking and jogging greatly benefit the cardio-vascular system. However, when taken to extreme, it can damage ligaments. Recently it has been suggested that alternating jogging and walking is the best form of exercise. Prior to exams, when the organized games are discontinued, a walking programme is best for the student. You can choose your own time between study periods, and know that, not only is it of recreational value, but it is also needed to keep you mentally fit.

Running on the Spot

This is simply a stationary form of jogging. It is most convenient and can be done indoors, so that you are not dependent on the weather. The amount of exercise required to maintain fitness is five sessions per week, each of 20 minutes duration, at a rate of 80 - 90 steps per minute (i.e. the right heel hits the floor 80 - 90 times per minute). Again, if you are not already fit, you should gradually work up to this level over several weeks.

In order that aerobic exercises be beneficial, large muscle groups of the body must be involved. Any exercise undertaken must be of a repetitive nature and be undertaken continuously for 20 minutes. The chosen exercise must be performed a minimum of three or four times per week.

Flexibility

Some people show amazing flexibility and can stretch, turn, and twist with ease. However, some exercises can greatly enhance body flexibility. Swimming and Disco Dancing are particularly beneficial, while any stretching-associated exercises will loosen and tone up slack muscles. Our bodies are less likely to be damaged during strenuous exercise as a result. Exercises which involve stretching and ensure flexibility should be undertaken daily, if possible, but twice weekly will suffice.

Toning-Up Exercises

If you don't have the facility for organised sport, or just lack the time, some of the following sample exercises may also be beneficial. Remember that it is essential to warm up for a few minutes before starting. In total a 10 - 12 minute workout will suffice. These toning-up exercises are good for maintaining firm muscle tone and giving your body a nice firm and trim appearance.

Partial Sit-ups

Method: Lie on your back, legs flat on the floor (knees straight) with arms by your side, palms down. Raise your head and shoulders until you can see the floor beneath your heels.
Repeat 10 times.
Benefits: This exercises the abdominal muscles and the muscles in front of the thighs.

Chest and Leg Raising

Method: Lie on your stomach, with arms by your side, palms upward, facing the floor. Lift shoulders and legs simultaneously from the floor and hold for a few seconds before returning to rest position.
Repeat 10 times.
Benefits: This exercise tones the backs of the thighs, the buttocks and the back muscles.

Twist

Method: Stand with feet about thirty centimetres apart. Using your arms, twist the upper part of your body and head around as far as you can from side to side, so that you can look behind you.
Repeat 10 times.

Benefits: This tones up and improves your waist.

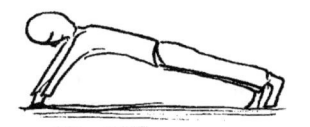

Push-Ups

Method: Lie on your stomach with your palms flat on the ground beneath your shoulders. Lift your body, keeping the back straight so that only your toes and palms touch the floor.
Return to resting position.
Repeat 10 times.

Benefits: Toning of upper trunk and arms.

6. ALCOHOL

15. ALCOHOL

Adolescence is generally regarded as a period of doubt and uncertainty. There is a desire during the teen years for young people to establish their own identity, combined with rejection of parental guidance. Young people tend to be influenced more by their peers than the older generation. While it is a time of physical growth, it is also a time for great emotional change. To help cope with their frustrations, alcohol is sometimes used by adolescents as a vehicle to transport them to an adult world, away from their childhood days. Standards are changing fast, and an educational system which causes many pressures, together with unemployment, may cause the youth to turn to alcohol as a means of escape.

Nowadays, it is generally accepted that most students drink. While adults have changed their attitude to drinking patterns, students still indulge heavily.

It is important to understand that alcohol in itself is not bad. Properly used, it can be enjoyable. Problems arise with alcohol when it is abused, i.e. when it is overused. When alcohol is being used properly it is always used sparingly and always only in social situations. Guidelines will be given later regarding the responsible handling of alcohol. When these guidelines are exceeded, one runs serious risk of suffering damaged health, both physical and mental, possibly leading to the horrors of alcoholism.

The past few years have seen a massive increase in the number of students who now consume alcoholic beverage on a regular basis. While curiosity may be the initial reason for trying alcohol, many students generally feel that they are not one of the "in crowd" unless they are part of the drinking set. Students meet to converse, exchange views, get acquainted, etc., in an environment which promotes the consumption of alcohol. Having a drink is perceived as being a mark of becoming an adult, of being in control, of being "cool". Many people feel it relaxes them and helps them to socialize. But alcohol is a central nervous system depressant. Higher controls are diminished, and this results in a feeling of elation, comraderie, and feelings of self-confidence. While alcohol may make one more chatty, it actually also makes one less in control. With excess alcohol there is a loss of timidity, the person will converse loudly with much gesticulation, and, at times, aggressive behaviour may occur in the form of rows, etc.

The effect of alcohol will depend on body weight, the stomach content, liver enzymes and the type of alcohol consumed.

In times past, description of the effects of alcohol intoxification went:

DRY + DELIGHTFUL

DELINQUENT + DISGUSTING

DAZED + DEJECTED

DEAD DRUNK

DEAD

1. Dry and delightful...................... ·1% alcohol in blood
2. Delinquent and disgusting .... ·2% alcohol in blood
3. Dazed and dejected .... ·3% alcohol in blood
4. Dead drunk .... ·4% alcohol in blood
5. Dead.. ·5% alcohol in blood

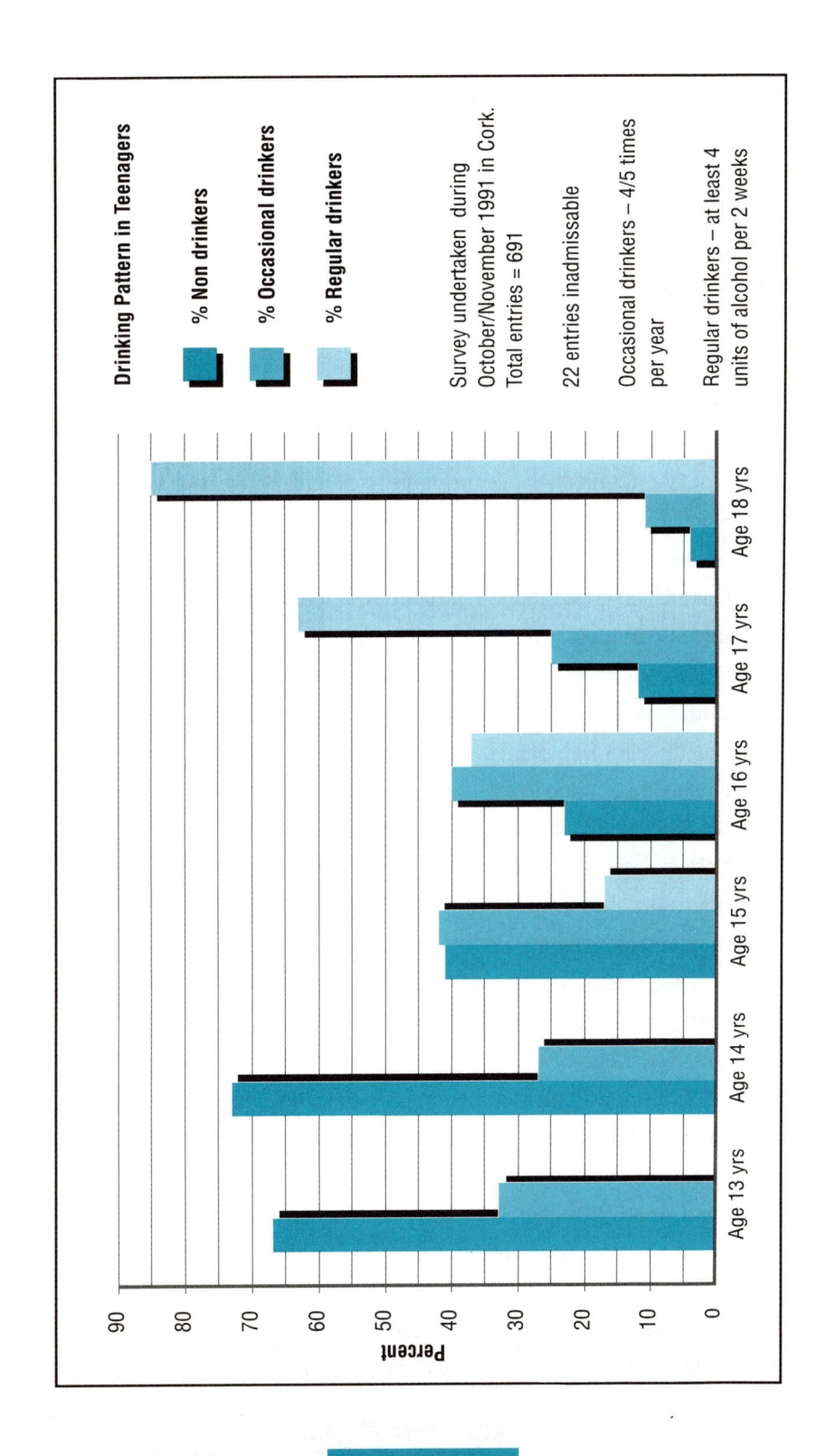

PHYSICAL AND PSYCHOLOGICAL EFFECTS OF ALCOHOL ABUSE

The physical and psychological effects of alcohol are widespread as it is distributed to all bodily organs and tissues. Excessive use leads to serious problems including the following:

1. It depresses the central nervous system.
2. It is addictive; larger quantities becoming necessary to get the (same) desired effect.
3. One is emotionally labile, unstable – elated and weepy.
4. Sleep disturbance, varying from insomnia on the one hand to excessive sleep on the other.
5. Diminished concentration, forgetfulness, confusion.
6. Increase in blood pressure, leading to headaches.
7. Motor movements are clumsy. Unsteady walk, loss of balance, slurred speech.
8. Gastritis, stomach pain, nausea and vomiting.
9. Flushed face – due to dilation of blood vessels.
10. Blackouts, difficulty in recalling events.
11. Behaviour changes may result in aggressive behaviour, both physically and verbally.
12. Impaired judgement.
13. Impaired social functioning – a tendency to be over-familiar with strangers, being loud and boisterous, inappropriate behaviour.
14. 10 - 25per cent of social drinkers will ultimately develop alcoholism, with all its adherent problems. Twenty-five percent of all new admissions to Psychiatric Hospitals are alcoholics. Children of alcoholics have a four-fold increase in their chance of developing the disease. Boys are more at risk than girls. Statistics show that being an alcoholic takes ten years off your life.

Many students who drink alcohol do so to the relieve social anxiety. These days, the educational system demands great commitment, resulting in the majority of students having had little time to improve their social skills. Students should realise that all their colleagues are in the same predicament as themselves. They also have limited socialising experience. Social inadequacy should be conquered by club/society/game participation. Relying on alcohol to ease social tension is fraught with danger.

ADVICE FOR STUDENTS WHO DRINK

RESPONSIBLE DRINKING — SECOND LEVEL
Teenagers younger than 16 years of age should not consume alcohol. Sixteen to eighteen year-old students should take very little alcohol, and

then only on special occasions, such as Christmas or the odd weekend. Two glasses of beer, or the equivalent, should be the maximum.

THIRD LEVEL

Restrict drinking to the weekends. Only drink during the week on special occasions, such as birthdays, weddings, etc. A couple of beers on the weekend would be a reasonable level of consumption. If you are drinking significantly more than this you are showing danger signs. On average, if you consume more than two pints, or the equivalent, at a single sitting you are beginning to cause physical damage.

General Points for Safe Drinking

1. Delay taking up drinking alcohol until as late an age as possible.
2. Avoid day-time drinking.
3. Drink when you are relaxed, and then in moderation. If you feel you must appear to be consuming alcohol, sip slowly.
4. Never drink on an empty stomach. Try to eat before and while drinking.
5. Drink only in social situations, surrounded by your friends.
6. Don't drink to help yourself perform socially.
7. Don't regard drinking alcohol as proof of adulthood.
8. Avoid peer pressure. Make your own decisions regarding your alcohol intake.
9. Control your alcohol intake and your finances by buying your own drinks. Actively discourage the "rounds" system.
10. Feel comfortable drinking soft drinks. Change to mineral water, non-alcoholic beverages, etc.
11. People who prefer non-alcoholic beverages should not become a source of amusement. They are independent thinkers.
12. Decide in advance the limit to the number of drinks you will have on a social occasion. Do not exceed that limit. Be strict with yourself.
13. Be aware of the danger of mixing alcohol with drugs, including prescribed medication.

14. Take your drink in an orderly fashion. Do not be tempted to get another drink at the counter while ordering.
15. Avoid spirits or use generous amounts of mixers (tonics/sodas).
16. Females should be aware that alcohol is more concentrated in their blood stream than in their male counterparts. The female body contains less water per unit bodyweight. Intoxification will, therefore, occur at a lower level.

CHANGING ATTITUDES

Over the past decade the Irish attitude to drinking alcohol has changed dramatically. Adults now rarely consume alcohol during the working day, and then only in moderation. Lunchtime indulgence is a thing of the past. People are more health conscious, and want to remain in control of their lives.

While £1.8 billion is still spent on alcohol annually, spirits have shown a marked decrease in sales. Mineral water and soft drinks are replacing alcohol in social situations.

Success and promotion at work never go hand in hand with excess alcoholic intake. Most heavy drinkers are now in the 40 - 50 age bracket. Upwardly mobile young professionals have become health conscious, and are concerned about diet, exercise etc. Alcohol has gone out of fashion with these young people, and soft drinks and mineral waters have become fashionable. The growth of the latter has been phenomenal. While still expensive, they are drug free, calorie free, caffeine free, and do give an image of being self-controlled.

Students undertaking second and third level education are highly motivated. They plan their future with great care. Dedicated work requires a period of relaxation, and a good social life is both necessary and beneficial. For the balanced person a few drinks will do no harm. On the other hand, young people with emotional difficulties should be aware of the consequences of abusing alcohol.

7. ADDICTIONS AND DRUG ABUSE

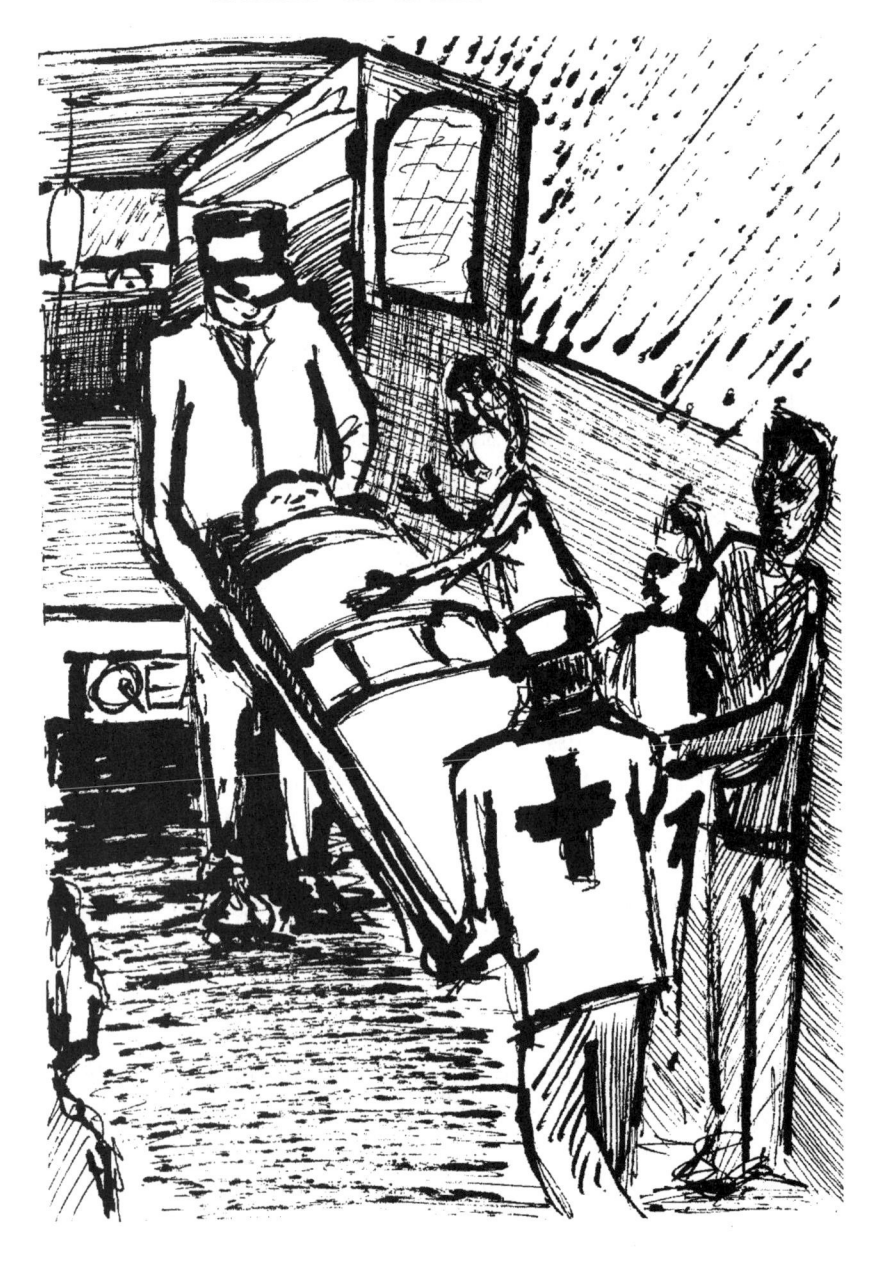

16. DRUG ABUSE

CIGARETTE SMOKING

Cigarette smoking is extremely common amongst the student population. Nicotine is the active substance involved. Although its popularity has decreased from an all time high of 41 per cent in the seventies, it still remains a serious health hazard. Cigarette smoking is closely associated with:

- Lung cancer. Cigarette smoking is a major causative factor in over 90 per cent of the 1700 deaths from lung cancer in Ireland each year
- Heart disease, heart attacks and increased cholesterol
- Lip and mouth cancers
- Pneumonia and bronchitis
- Circulatory problems – 80 per cent of people with these are smokers

Cigarette smoking is an appallingly unhealthy habit that is still being taken up by young people. It is evident that, even with education and changing attitudes towards smoking, teenagers are still not impressed with statistics about illnesses which occur in later life.

FACTS ABOUT TEENAGE SMOKING

- At the age of 10 years, 3 per cent of girls and 8 per cent of boys smoke more than one cigarette per day.
- During teenage years there is a gradual but steady increase in smoking in both sexes, with males predominating.
- At the age of 16 years, in both sexes, 31 per cent smoke regularly.
- Of the 31 per cent who smoke, 34 per cent have tried to give up smoking.
- 85 per cent of adolescent smokers would welcome a Health Education programme in the school/college.

Marlene Dietrich (*Courtesy of The Kobal Collection, London*)

FACTS ABOUT COLLEGE STUDENTS

A survey of student smoking habits in third level education was recently undertaken in a Cork College.

A questionnaire was issued randomly to students attending the Student Health Office over a period of three weeks.

Overall 500 questionnaires were issued, 470 were completed satisfactorily. 290 females and 180 males returned the completed forms.

It was found that   26% of female students smoke.

30% of male students smoke.

Of the 500 students surveyed:

15% smoked 1 - 10 cigarettes per day.

9.5% smoked 10- 20 cigarettes per day.

1.5% smoked 20+ cigarettes per day.

FACTS ABOUT ADULT SMOKERS

1. 30% of adults smoke cigarettes regularly.
2. 75% of adults have tried cigarettes.
3. 70% of smokers would like to give up the smoking habit.
4. In adult life females smoke more than males.

In former times cigarette smoking was seen to be socially sophisticated. Only in the last 20 years has it been established that cigarettes are physically damaging to your health. In the old movies of Humphrey Bogart and Marlene Dietrich one sees the latter surrounded by wisps of smoke, staring provocatively at the camera. They seemed so elegant, dangling a cigarette in one hand, while fingering an ashtray with the other. They had an aura of casual sophistication about them. They were glamorous, mysterious and chic. People were influenced by such imagery, and cigarette smoking became a "with it" thing to do. Nobody seemed influenced by the fact that Humphrey Bogart died of cancer of the throat.

Today we know that the long-term effects of cigarette smoking far outweigh the social benefits. The smoker is now more likely to be perceived as being nervous. In reality smokers tend to be somewhat socially insecure and anxious. A student will often take up cigarette smoking as a social prop. They will use the cigarette to relax them a little and give them something to do with their hands. These facts are fairly widely known, and so the smoker would now be less likely to be seen as "cool" and more likely to be seen as more vulnerable and socially unsure.

The following table illustrates the detrimental effects of smoking on both appearance and health.

- Headaches
- Frequent colds, flu
- Bad breath
- Decreased blood pressure
- Rarely physically fit
- Increased tooth decay
- Nausea
- Skin ages faster (Increased tendency to wrinkle)
- Excess sweating
- Poor concentration
- Staining of Teeth and Fingernails
- Weight gain on giving up smoking

If you take a serious view of your education, then you should absorb these facts which will help you to avoid cigarette smoking altogether. You will also avoid much pain and suffering in later years.

For several years now the Department of Health has educated us about the hazards of cigarette smoking. Yet thousands of students continue to take up the habit, thereby damaging their health and consequently the prospects for their future. Nicotine is a drug, and dependency quickly develops. A cigarette or two will become a packet. The average smoker consumes 20 cigarettes a day.

Lest anyone doubt that smoking is not addictive, simply watch what happens when the smoker stops and the unpleasant withdrawal symptoms appear.

In the early stages when the teenager smokes a cigarette or two it brings about a temporary relaxation which is pleasurable. However, to continue to acquire this feeling one must increase, like all addictions, the amount of nicotine taken. So one or two cigarettes per day will then become ten. Peer pressure is usually part of the problem, and for some unknown reason school children think that it is a sign of maturity to be a smoker. In former times it was regarded also as a "rebellious" act, but recent studies have shown that smokers are more immature and socially unsure of themselves than non-smokers. An added attraction to girls appears to be that smoking can decrease appetite, and so they use it as a weight reducer. A further complication, known for some time, is that cigarette smoking and alcohol intake tend to go together. In a recent survey of second level students in Cork, 78% of smokers drank regularly. Another 17% drank on special occasions, and only 5% did not drink at all. The non-smokers, on the other hand, presented an entirely different picture. Only 16% drank regularly. A further 40% drank on special occasions such as Christmas/Anniversaries (once/twice a year). The remainder never took alcohol. Most recent surveys show that smoking and alcohol go hand in hand.

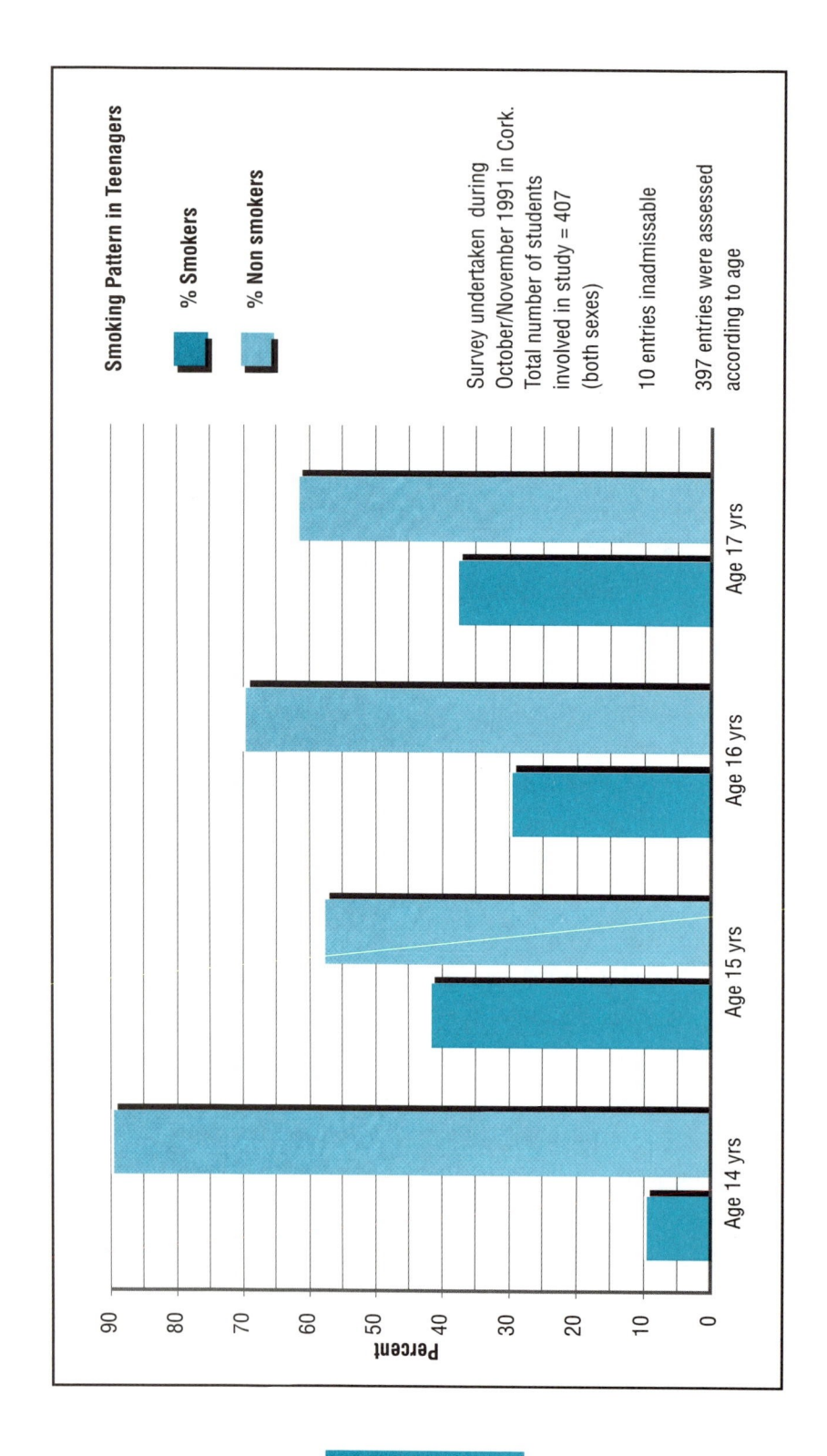

Smoking Pattern in Teenagers

■ % Smokers

■ % Non smokers

Survey undertaken during October/November 1991 in Cork.
Total number of students involved in study = 407 (both sexes)

10 entries inadmissable

397 entries were assessed according to age

PASSIVE SMOKERS

Most non-smokers are aware that even though they themselves do not indulge in this dangerous habit, they consume nicotine by being in an atmosphere containing tobacco. Therefore, they risk suffering the same ill-effects, although the risk is lower, as previously outlined for the smoker. They also suffer from a range of superficial ill effects. Intense discomfort can be caused by effects ranging from eye irritation, and running nose, to throat problems and pain. Effects vary with age, some being particularly susceptible. An increased awareness of these facts has made people less tolerant of the smoker, and they will quickly point out the "No Smoking" signs in public places. Non-smokers, when asked "Do you mind if I smoke?" should make their feelings known. What is the point in being a non-smoker if you put yourself at risk by allowing the smoker to persist in endangering your health?   Be firm.

HOW TO STOP SMOKING

Surveys show that 70 per cent of adult smokers would like to stop. However, one must realise that it is extremely difficult to "kick the habit". Like any other addiction, there are numerous unpleasant withdrawal symptoms to endure. It is not easy, but the sooner one commits oneself to stopping the better. Some studies have shown that a gradual slowing down process can be beneficial, but if one is really determined one should:

1. Choose a day to stop smoking completely.
2. Do not cut down gradually – stop completely.
3. Be determined and inflexible.
4. Tell all your friends that you have stopped smoking.
5. Use relaxation techniques to overcome tension and irritability.
6. Reward yourself for success, e.g. use the money saved to buy yourself a new book or clothes, etc. Contract with yourself to do something really special after three months of not smoking.

Realise:
1. That craving will occur.
2. That one must expect to be agitated, restless and anxious.
3. That insomnia may occur.
4. That one's appetite may increase with a resulting weight gain of approximately two kilos.

Important

Do not let the thought "I can't smoke" get you down. Such a negative and self-pitying attitude will make you feel deprived. Giving up smoking doesn't mean the end of socializing. You must accept you will have that desire to indulge for months. Smoking associated situations, e.g. meals, bars, discos, having a coffee, will bring back that old familiar feeling.

Be prepared. However, do realise you are making a conscious decision each time you smoke. Pause and ask yourself on each occasion, "Will I smoke"? You are making the ultimate decision. You are responsible and in control. You are making your choice. Quitting smoking is worth the effort. Weigh up the pros and the cons as you ask yourself, "Will I smoke"?

CANNABIS

Cannabis is obtained from the plant Cannabis Saliva, and is usually smoked when mixed with tobacco. Amongst the student population there may be a small sub-group in the school or college who indulge. The national percentage of abusers is not known, and a recent survey of 16-year olds in Cork revealed that 6.1per cent had participated in taking Cannabis just once or twice. There were no regular users.

Most teenagers like to promote Cannabis as having a euphoric effect. It can, however, precipitate panic attacks and confusional states, and it gives the user a feeling of laxity and drowsiness. Its effects last approximately 2 - 4 hours. Chronic users, on the other hand, commonly develop an "Amotivational Syndrome", e.g. becoming disinterested in school or college, in fact anything that requires prolonged attention is rejected. The user will become listless, gain weight and is generally slowed down. They are passive and lacking in ambition. They rarely take the required school or college exams, ultimately dropping out of their studies altogether.

SEDATIVES

Ativan, Librium and Valium are a group of minor tranquillisers that are sometimes abused by young people. One can also include in this group, barbiturates such as Seconal, Mandrax and cough mixtures of various sorts. In general, these cause sedation in various degrees, and some, if abused, bring about disorientation, confusion and slurred speech. Effects of overdose would include breathing difficulty, decrease in body temperature, dilated pupils, rapid heart rate, and possible *death*.

They carry a degree of both physical and psychological dependency. Effects may last from two to 24 hours.

STIMULANTS

This category of drugs would include Cocaine ("Coke", "Flake" or Snow"), Amphetamines ("Purple Hearts", "Speed", Caffeine and weight reducing drugs such as Ponderax, Tenuate). This group of stimulants carry the highest degree of psychological dependency of all drugs. Their effects may last from an hour to five hours, and the usual method of taking them would be either orally or by injection. Effects, short and long-term, would include an increased degree of alertness, excitement, increased heart rate and blood pressure, chronic insomnia, and loss of appetite and weight loss. Body temperature may rise. The effects may include hallucinations and convulsions, and possible *death*.

OPIATES

Analgesics such a Pethadine, Codeine and Morphine are in this group. Also included are Opium and Heroin. Heroin may be used in the form of "Horse" or "Smack". Opiates carry a high degree of physical dependency in addition to a high degree of psychological dependency. The duration of effects may be from two hours to 24 hours, and they may be used by oral means or injected into the bloodstream. Their possible effects would include elation, mood changes varying from elation to drowsiness, respiratory difficulties, constrictal eye pupil, nausea, vomiting, and a possible decrease in body temperature. Long-term abuse will ultimately lead to convulsions and *death*.

HALLUCINOGENS

L.S.D. and inhalents are in this group. They will produce illusions, delusions and hallucinations. The person is not aware of the passage of time. "Trip" episodes on L.S.D. can result in psychotic behaviour; chronic abuse can result in death. Inhalents such as glues, petrol, aerosols and other volatile substances, e.g. Bensene are also hallucinogens and carry the same side-effects.

In Conclusion

Young people who participate in drug abuse are being exploited by pushers for great financial gain. These pushers feed off the inadequacies of the young, providing them with addictive drugs, most of which are life threatening. Robberies, car thefts, credit card fraud, etc., are all used to finance the user's growing addiction. Great work is being undertaken by Social Workers, Teachers, the Clergy and Gardai to cope with this growing problem.

Treatment centres are provided by all Health Boards. Should you have a problem with drug abuse, you should contact your local General Practitioner. He/she will see you confidentially and seek a service suitable to your needs.

8. GUIDE FOR PARENTS OF TEENAGERS

17. GUIDE FOR PARENTS

Students' results depend not only on the student, but also on the family with whom they live. The parents, brothers, and sisters, all play a major part in the student's development.

Most students develop socially, psychologically and physically over the teenage years without any particular trauma. Parents expect the usual mood swings, excitements, bouts of aggression, indecision, anxiety, etc. as part and parcel of these vulnerable years. They see their child grow from a clinging offspring to a young, independent adult.

However, in order to participate positively in the student's life and to offer constructive help and guidance, parents must be aware of the anxieties of young people generally. These include:

- Social anxieties. They have a fear of being rejected by peers, of being ignored, of being criticized, of having difficulty conversing, and of being unable to establish boyfriend/girlfriend relationships
- Having difficulty communicating with parents. A strained relationship with one parent
- Family insecurities and problems, lack of finance, unemployment, alcoholism, etc.
- Fear of educational failure
- Being rejected by teachers
- Being unattractive, fat, worried about acne. Concern about wearing the right clothes
- Lack of sporting acumen. Being embarrassed by lack of skill
- Sexual doubts. Delayed secondary sexual characteristics in boys (a delay of three years is not unusual). They may develop fears of being homosexual. Explanation and reassurance from parents and/or G.P. is necessary for these students
- Difficulty in making decisions and difficulty gaining independence from their parents

A parent's role is indeed a difficult one. On the one hand they must be in control of the family unit, and on the other hand be a provider, counsellor, teacher and friend, all rolled into one. The vast majority of parents do a splendid job. Disagreements about going out, hairstyles, friends, clothes, discos, etc. are ultimately negotiated on. There is always a certain degree of flexibility to be found that will bring happiness to all.

GENERAL HOME RULES

General rules apply to us all, likewise to your children. While house rules may differ from family to family, in each situation they will have been clearly established over a long period of time. When your child becomes a teenager, he/she will have observed how these rules apply to the family unit, and what behaviour is expected of him/her.

House rules must be clearly stated by parents. One must be consistent. Never make idle threats. House rules should be negotiated on, when possible, to avoid conflict. Always let your children know the rules well in advance, so that if they are broken, they will be aware of the consequences of their actions. If a major rule is ignored, physical punishment is never the answer as it will make the gap between parent and child even wider. Instead, teenagers should be grounded, have reduction in their pocket money, or have an increase in household chores. Keep calm and always ensure the communication lines remain open.

Adolescents should be involved in all family decisions. This does not simply mean deciding on the family holiday. They should be aware of financial limitations, illnesses, choice of schools, expectations of family members, etc. Parents must listen to adolescents and be aware of social happenings. They should be prepared to discuss alcohol, smoking, Aids, drug abuse, etc. Most parents find discussing matters of a sexual nature embarrassing and at times stressful. Usually they leave this to the school authorities, the newspapers or indeed chat shows. This is sad as it leaves the teenager with inadequate and, at times, faulty information. It is best to be casual and communicate openly on such matters. Beginning is half the battle. Once you start you will find it amazing how easily the conversation flows. A close relationship with your children will mean they can approach you in later years when more personal problems arise.

Understand that all children think that their parents are old-fashioned, and out of touch. Be aware that they are of a different generation, style, fashion, etc.

Know their friends. Encourage them to invite them to the house. Help to organise study groups by providing snacks, etc. You should know where your children are, but not to the point of being over inquisitive. At this stage adolescents may keep a diary of a personal nature – you must resist the temptation to inform yourself. Likewise never listen on the telephone or open letters. Respect their privacy, and give them space.

PARENTS' ROLE DURING SCHOOL TERM

Parents love their children, want them to succeed and to be content. Their task is to help them to become responsible adults. This includes motivating and assisting them throughout the school year. Up to the end of primary school all parents are very familiar with the classroom situation. They attend school meetings, oversee homework, etc. However, once their children enter secondary school there is a gradual withdrawal of general support. There is little explanation for this other than:

- The adolescents now demand less attention than their younger siblings. They are also capable of getting study done alone, etc.
- Parents equate physical growth with psychological growth, which is not necessarily the same thing.
- Many parents find it easier to relate to younger children. Some may feel impatient, embarrassed or irritated by the issues and problems of the teenage years.
- Poor discipline may result in the teenager drifting away from the family unit and getting involved in troublesome or anti-social behaviour.

In recent years, the educational system demands such results, that parents must participate in their adolescents' education if they want them to succeed. Everyone can find fault with the present system, but we must learn to work with it and use it to our advantage. You should make yourself familiar with the various aspects of the educational system. Know the subjects available at school, in particular those chosen by your child. Assist him/her in the difficult decision of choosing subjects. The teachers will gladly discuss previous exam grades and together you can decide what choices of subjects are the most suitable.

Be realistic. All children are different even within the same family. Some may be very academic, others may shine at non-academic subjects. Discuss your child's ambitions. Remember to keep as many options open as possible to third level education. Make sure they are not missing out on a vital subject. If it appears that the level of points expected would not allow them to get a profession, then encourage them to look positively at other career prospects. Help them to decide whether to go on to third level education or to find a career more appropriate to their talents at the end of second level. Nowadays, there are a wide range of careers available to them. Get involved in considering everything before narrowing down the choices.

STUDY ENVIRONMENT

The student is so involved with the business of school/college/university, that his/her parents should make it their business to provide a healthy study environment. The following guidelines should be met:

(a) The student should occupy the same quiet room, as far removed from family activity (e.g. TV, radio) as possible.

(b) The desk/study table should be placed away from distractions, e.g. windows.

(c) The bench should measure a minimum of 50 x 100 cm. The accompanying chair should be firm backed.

(d) The area should be well lit. A desk lamp is essential to avoid eye strain. This should be placed on the opposite side to the hand with which the student writes so as to avoid shadows.

(d) Ensure that the room is warm and comfortable. Stuffiness causes headaches. A window should remain slightly open.

(e) All equipment and books should be available on shelves nearby.

(f) If the room is to be tidied, avoid moving books and notes.
Near exam time it may be best for parents to avoid the study room altogether!

STUDY HOURS

A good study plan is essential. It not only organises study time to the best advantage, but actually reduces the amount of time that the student will have to spend on study. See Chapter 5 on "Using Precious Time Wisely".

Students should arrive home as soon as possible after school, except when there are planned activities, e.g. sport, music, etc. They should take the main meal of the day with the entire family. The general events of the day for all should be discussed. Students taking exams should be encouraged to discuss how they are getting on. Advice should be given in a practical and informal way.

They should be ready to commence study at 6 p.m., or not later than 6.30 p.m. if the meal cannot be finished earlier. The students themselves will know about concentration difficulties and the need to take short breaks (see Chapter 2). However, a 15-20 minute break should be planned for 8.30 p.m. This may mean taking a snack, calling a friend, watching some T.V. ,etc. Study should be resumed on time, and finish at 10.00 p.m. At exam time they may wish to extend this until 11.00 p.m. One should certainly advise against study after midnight.

It is essential to take time from study each week to relax and develop other important areas. As a general rule Sundays should be free, with one other free evening (e.g. Wednesday night) and one other free half day (e.g. Saturday morning or afternoon). Students should plan these times to fit in with their own requirements – sports, cinema, etc.

DIET

A good, healthy diet is composed of protein, carbohydrates, fat, vitamins, minerals and fibre, all in the right proportions. Choosing a diet that will supply the student with nutrients in optimum proportions is very easy indeed. The choice is governed by the first and most important law of good nutrition and healthy living. This says that one should eat a diet that is consistently varied across the four major food groups (Dairy group, Fruit and Vegetable group, Cereal group and Meats and Beans group). See Chapter 12 for details.

Most teenagers love take-away fast foods. These are fatty foods and should not be taken to excess. Make sure the student's main meal of the day is taken with the family and is as leisurely as possible. If lunch is taken to school, make sure it is varied and attractive.

PHYSICAL EXERCISE

The student should have a moderate amount of aerobic exercise. This should be pursued throughout the school year. However, as the last term of the year draws near, students may insist on discarding their organised school games. A simple regime of some other form of exercise, as suggested in Chapter 14 , will suffice.

MOTIVATION

Once the student has decided on a set career, the motivation to acquire the necessary results is usually self-sustaining. They can look forward to a career of their own choosing. They should be realistic about their choice, which is usually based on past performance. Perhaps if it is placed a little higher, that is a good thing in itself. It gives them the necessary spur and will egg them on to higher things. However, parents should encourage students to attain the ambitions by encouraging them gently, taking each day at a time. Do not instil your own fears on the student, or you will overwhelm them with anxiety. All students will understand that a successful end to second level education will be their passport to a secure and happy future. If a student shows an interest in a specific subject or career, parents should try to obtain the necessary information for them. Likewise, should you buy a book on a particular aspect of their studies, they will be pleased. As the exam draws nearer, pay special attention to the students' needs. He/she may require more time to study. Make sure other family members are aware of his/her dilemma and that emphasis is placed on their predicament. The family should learn to adapt to this temporary situation by realising that the student needs space and silence, and can no longer be expected to undertake household chores as he/she once did.

If parents have expertise in any particular subject they should offer help. If not, they should still offer help in the form of asking questions, participating in "mock orals", etc. They should provide students with editorials from the newspapers. This will be necessary to improve their English and help them through their oral examinations. Give them ideas for essays. If your child feels that he/she is falling behind in any subject, encourage him/her to ask advice of the teacher involved, outside of class. A grind may be the solution.

THE EXAMINATION ITSELF

The parent should obtain the necessary equipment for the examination for the students, who are now too busy to go and acquire it themselves, e.g. calculator, ruler, mathematical set, pencils, etc.

The timetable should be carefully assessed four weeks in advance. At a quick glance one should know what subject is on a particular day, and what time the exam actually commences and ends, etc.

On the morning of the first subject one must expect the student to be anxious and very preoccupied with the forthcoming exam. Be supportive and calm. If the student wishes to discuss the subject, be prepared to do so in an encouraging way. Point out that he/she has worked hard and that you feel that he/she is ready to take this exam.

When they get home in the evening have a special meal prepared. Make sure the exam is the centre of attention. Look at the exam paper, carefully discussing each question undertaken. Discuss their views, their disappointments and hopes. For state exams, discuss the national view of exam subjects by relating to the newspaper summary. Tell them that it doesn't matter what their friends felt about the paper as this was a national exam. Cheer them up! Let them talk out the paper for approximately 30 minutes, and then gradually divert their attention to general family matters. The main meal should be as relaxed as possible. If there is a crisis of any sort, discuss it privately. Suggest to the student that they should glance over notes on the next subject for approximately one hour. Praise them for a day's work well done.

They may be over excited by the day's happenings. Get them to ease off gradually. An early night, with parental reassurance, will be all the therapy they need.

SUGGESTIONS FOR PARENTS

1. Discuss school problems with the adolescent.
2. Discuss his/her personal and social problems.
3. Discuss adolescent changes, such as menstruation, etc.
4. Discuss physical and psychological changes of the life cycle (childhood to old age), i.e. normal development.
5. Discuss diet and physical exercise.

6. Negotiate and set house rules. Be consistent in applying sanctions. Keep communication lines open.
7. Discuss social rules regarding discos, outings, etc.
8. Help choose ideal weight for age, sex and height.
9. Limit carbohydrate foods but do not dismiss them from the diet. Do not allow over-emphasis on carbohydrate foods.
10. Avoid very large helpings.
11. Should the student become diet conscious and lose weight, seek immediate help and get medical advice.

PARENTS' GUIDE TO STUDENTS AT RISK

Behaviour changes in students at risk include the following:
1. Staying in their room for prolonged periods (beyond time on their study plan).
2. Emotional instability (crying spells, marked mood swings).
3. Aggressive outbursts, physical and verbal.
4. Being secretive about activities.
5. Having extra money.
6. Stealing, or selling personal articles.
7. Problems at school (unable to compete, dropping grades, truancy).
8. Staying out late.
9. Strange new friends.
10. Weight loss, not interested in food, poor appetite.
11. Appearing drunk, being drowsy, generalized fatigue, lack of energy.

Always discuss any such changes with the adolescent. Seek professional advice if the problem is not resolved.